Pink-pilled

Manchester University Press

Pink-pilled

Women and the far right

Lois Shearing

Manchester University Press

Published by Manchester University Press
Oxford Road, Manchester, M13 9PL
www.manchesteruniversitypress.co.uk

British Library Cataloguing-in-Publication Data
A catalogue record for this book is available from the British Library

ISBN 978 1 5261 7069 9 paperback

First published 2024

The publisher has no responsibility for the persistence or accuracy of
URLs for any external or third-party internet websites referred to in
this book, and does not guarantee that any content on such websites is,
or will remain, accurate or appropriate.

EU authorised representative for GPSR:
Easy Access System Europe – Mustamäe tee 50, 10621 Tallinn, Estonia
gpsr.requests@easproject.com

Typeset in 10.5/14.5 Trump Mediaeval LT Std
by Cheshire Typesetting Ltd, Cuddington, Cheshire

For the anti-fascists
And for Alex, for putting up with all this

Are you a bad person, or do you just have reasonable concerns, are you a bad person, or are you just asking questions? In the crushed heat death you ask how to win a culture war, and when does a culture war become a real war, where is the line that is crossed, is it the spilling of blood and has blood already spilled? It must be a war to be called a war.

Alison Rumfitt, *Tell Me I'm Worthless*

Under tyranny, most friends are a liability. One quarter of them turn 'reasonable' and become your enemies, one quarter are afraid to stop and speak, and one quarter are killed and you die with them. But the blessed final quarter keep you alive.

Sinclair Lewis, *It Can't Happen Here*

Contents

Introduction

Are women more conservative than men?

I was surprised to open Andrea Dworkin's *Right-Wing Women* to find that the controversial feminist theorist had started her influential text by considering a similar question. Dworkin speculates that women are thought to be 'biologically conservative' because their reproductive capabilities leave them vulnerable and therefore less inclined to take the risks necessary to propel society forwards. Paraphrasing male academics and commenters (indeed, men in general), she notes that women have babies because that is what women do, a fact of life that carries with it the obligation to nurture, raise and protect those babies. 'Therefore, women can be expected to be socially, politically, economically, and sexually conservative because the status quo, whatever it is, is safer than change, whatever the change.'[1]

Dworkin sets out to explore the politics of conservative and ultra-right-wing women, and ultimately concludes that they are the result of patriarchal conditioning as opposed to being biologically determined. Hers was one of the first books to examine women on the right, taking their political beliefs and activism seriously, as opposed to writing it off as a frivolous hobby, as so many of the male writers who preceded her did. If Dworkin were alive today, she and I might find ourselves in very different, perhaps even opposing, feminist camps, so I was prepared to disagree with some of her analysis (and indeed I did). But I was not expecting to be taken aback by the opening premise. I had spent most of my life assuming women were more prone to progressive thinking, acceptance of differences and support for bodily autonomy.

I wasn't alone in thinking this. The far right believes this about women too. We differ in that they see it as a flaw in (white) women; white women, they claim, are fair and gentle creatures – 'the fairer sex'. Therefore, white women must be protected from themselves in order to save the West. White women, tricked by their maternal nature, want to take in and care for those fleeing violence in their own countries. So, their right to vote (and the possibility that they might vote for leaders with progressive views about immigration) must be taken from them. White women are degenerate liberals; they tolerate homosexuality and take innocent white children to drag brunches. White women are sluts; they sleep with chads all throughout college, having abortion after abortion, before tricking some 'beta simp' – a term used in the 'manosphere' to refer to supposedly weak men who don't subscribe to their worldview – into marrying them. I have seen these arguments – sometimes blending together into a singular post where white women are simultaneously hailed as 'mother warriors' and 'cumbuckets' – made over and over again in the three years I spent researching the far right for this project.

Research also supports the notion that women skew more progressive than their male counterparts. For example, in 2023 the American polling firm Change Research found that women under 50 were more likely to describe themselves as progressive or liberal (58 per cent in total for women aged 18–35 and 44 per cent in total for women aged 35–49, with 29 per cent in the latter category describing themselves as 'moderate'[2]). Men in those age ranges were much more polarised. In the over fifties categories, however, there was much less of a divide across genders: while women aged 40–64 were slightly more likely to describe themselves as progressives or moderate, the split was almost even for men and women over 65. Women skew slightly more progressive on a number of specific issues too, including abortion (in 2022, 64 per cent of American women said they identified as pro-choice, compared to 61 per cent of men, according to Pew Research Center),[3] same-sex marriage,[4] equality for transgender people[5] and climate change.[6]

But this hasn't always been the case. As we'll explore further in Chapter 1, women have historically been reliable voters for right-wing and conservative parties, particularly during the postwar period. Several theories have been suggested to explain why this shift happened, including that women began entering higher education in droves in the late twentieth century – and are now more likely to attend tertiary education and earn a degree than men – and better-educated individuals are more likely to vote progressively. Political scientists Ronald Inglehart and Pippa Norris suggest that this shift can best be described as a generational process, one in which younger women who have experienced higher workforce participation, higher wages and less restrictive gender roles move leftward of the men in their party.[7]

Of course, not all women have shifted leftward. Some have ideologically stagnated, appearing more conservative as their peers moved towards more progressive ideals. Others still have moved right, joining the ranks of the men in their generation who have done the same. It is with these women that this book is concerned. I seek to understand why some women have broken off from their generational peers to join deeply misogynist far-right, neo-Nazi and white nationalist movements. How and where are they radicalised? Has the internet facilitated their radicalisation, like it has for so many young men? If so, how similar is the process for men and women? These are the questions this book examines, through a mixture of digging into the latest research and original reporting.

I was also blinkered to this form of benevolent sexism by my own access to white womanhood, believing women to be more progressive. I have never been on the receiving end of white women's hatred, tendency towards violence or desire for power. In many ways, I have both benefited from and perpetuated it. While I identify as genderfluid, I still move through the world being treated as a white woman and therefore have access to the systematic power of white womanhood. (For this reason, I have used the pronoun 'we' throughout this book when referring to white womanhood as an institution and 'they' to refer to womanhood as a gender identity that overlaps with mine but with which I do not fully identify.) Jessie Daniels, an expert on internet manifestations of racism, explores this in her book *Nice White Ladies: The Truth about White Supremacy, Our Role in It, and How We Can Help Dismantle It*.[8] She breaks down the ways in which civility and appeals to authority have become the weapons of choice of white womanhood, allowing white women to maintain a veneer of innocence and even progressiveness while weaponising a system designed to protect our comfort, even at the cost of the lives of people of colour. Therefore, white women play an instrumental role in the upkeep of white supremacy.

When I started this project, I did so because I couldn't find a satisfying answer to the question: why do women align themselves with movements that so clearly hate and harm them? Why do they advocate against their own rights and bodily autonomy? Why do they preach submission at the cost of their own wellbeing? Having spent a lot of my teens seeking out manosphere content and seeing the vitriolic hatred men have for

women, I couldn't understand why women were joining the ranks of the alt-right, which had in part grown
out of it. Was this some kind of false consciousness?
How could they disavow feminism while reaping its
benefits for their cause?

As I have come to discover, there is no single answer
to these questions. The reasons women seek out, fall
into or join far-right and white nationalist movements
are as varied as the women themselves. For many, it is
about aligning themselves with the domination of their
whiteness over the marginalisation of their womanhood;
while the far right and white nationalism may tell them
they are inferior to white men, it positions them above
everyone else. White nationalism and the far right offer
them an opportunity to reclaim the power they feel is
their birthright as *white* yet denied to them as *women*.

For others, it's about finding the community that
they have been searching for (these types of people are
referred to as 'seekers' in literature around radicalisation). Others still have a genuine belief that a woman's
role is to be subservient to men: whether by divine design
or the natural order. Some, frankly, are grifters, profiteering from hate through technocapitalist-designed
social media algorithms which reward polarisation. If
other types of content could promise them the same
levels of fame (or notoriety), following, power and
money without obliging them to compete in saturated
spaces such as fitness, beauty or even mommy blogging, they would be run-of-the-mill influencers rather
than white power propagandists.

The methods through which these women discover far-right and alt-right content online both overlap with and differ from men's experiences. Many women are 'red-pilled' (a slang term for becoming radicalised) through the same processes and internet pipelines as men: be it anti-feminism, white nationalism or anti-immigration, to name just a few. Others come through pipelines which appeal more specifically to women: tradwives, transphobia, natalism and new-age wellness. This difference, in which women are radicalised by other women, and the content and issues used to do so, I have come to refer to as 'pink-pilling', although this is not necessarily a term they use for themselves.

'Pink-pilling' as a term is embraced by the small community of self-identified 'femcels', an offshoot of women in the incel community (although, despite using the 'cel' suffix, many of the women in the movement distance themselves from incels, whom they identify as violent misogynists).[9] 'Femcel' is a loosely defined term and one that has outgrown its origins to become a faux-ironic self-identifier for young women in the digital 'girlblogging' subculture. We'll meet some of them later. The term 'pink-pilling' as well as 'femcel' can be traced back to Reddit, particularly to the r/Trufemcels subreddit, which at its peak had at least 25,000 members.[10] After the subreddit was banned in 2021, as part of the platform's attempt to clean up toxic speech, some members moved to a dedicated platform called PinkPilled.co,[11] although the site is no longer active at time of writing.

Women in white nationalist and far/alt-right movements tend to refer to themselves 'red-pilled', like their male counterparts. Others, most notably those radicalised by transphobia, refer to themselves as 'peaked'.[12] In this book, we'll explore multiple ways in which women are peaked and pilled, the ways in which these movements seek to appeal to them, and what women feel they have to gain from joining. We'll also explore how women are treated once they've joined those movements.

Finding an answer to why women are attracted to the far right doesn't provide a simple method for dissuading them. Unlike a lot of the perceived frustrations of men in these communities, including the loss of power as white men in an increasingly multicultural society and the loss of access to women that they feel entitled to, the pain-points being exploited to radicalise women are rooted in their marginalisation. Far-right ideology and propaganda is dialectical: it positions whiteness as both naturally stronger and superior to all others, while simultaneously being in a state of perpetual victimhood – attacked and marginalised through increased immigration and diversity initiatives.

Women, most notably white women but also cis, straight, able-bodied, naturalised women, do occupy a position of both power over others and marginalisation. Because of this, it can be difficult to try to persuade women away from radicalisation pipelines without appearing to side with the systems that oppress them. Take the increasingly common talking point that

8

women's entry into the workforce was not a feminist victory but a victory for the state looking to increase its income tax earnings, and that women were happier as housewives or stay-at-home mothers. When arguing against this, we must be careful not to align ourselves with a capitalist system that also oppresses women, underpaying and overworking them compared to their male counterparts. Instead, we must align our arguments with a type of feminism that seeks women's liberation from those oppressive systems, rather than inclusion in them.

Of course, the reasons men adopt far-right views are also varied and complex, and there are genuine systemic forces at play, notably economic ones. But there has been a huge amount of attention, writing, reporting and research dedicated to men's radicalisation. When the alt-right began to make waves in the mid-2000s, headline after headline decried an apparent epidemic of teenage boys being radicalised in gaming lobbies or pick-up forums. Otherwise, they extolled the charm of a new kind of fascist, those such as Richard Spencer or Milo Yiannopoulos, with journalists apparently agog that a white supremacist could also have table manners and a received pronunciation (RP) accent.

When the alt-right began to step out into the street and become overtly murderous, the actions and motivations of so-called lone wolf terrorists and militias such as the Proud Boys understandably filled the headlines. This wave of media attention culminated in the 6 January insurrection, when Trump supporters and varying far-right groups stormed the Capitol Building. But far fewer column inches and research papers have been dedicated to the women who have played instrumental if (arguably) indirect roles in the sharp increase in far-right violence and spread of far-right politics.

This book builds on existing research and reporting, as well as my own original reporting from 18 months spent monitoring places where far-right communities gather online, including in private Telegram channels, forums, Facebook groups, Instagram, X (formerly Twitter) and Tumblr, Pinterest, as well as Gab and Truth Social to a lesser extent.

To do this, I adopted the alias of Ava White, a 23-year-old cisgender, straight, white, British woman from the south-east who is single, unemployed and worried about rising immigration in her area as well the threat of trans women in what she considers 'women's spaces'. Armed with an old handset, a prepaid SIM card and a virtual private network (VPN), I set up accounts for Ava across various social media sites, including Instagram, X, Facebook, Gab, YouTube, and Truth Social. I also created a Telegram account for Ava, which proved to be one of the most fruitful: as Ava I monitored around 15 Telegram channels, most of which were monodirectional, run by some of the key members of the British far-right, as well as large anonymous channels dedicated to sharing far-right memes, propaganda and talking points. It was in these channels that I learned the most about how the far right operates online, when they believe to be talking among themselves rather than to a wider audience. Here, they argued with each other, spoke openly about their beliefs and posted updates about their lives.

Over the course of this book, I explore why we should be concerned with women's involvement in the far right, despite the fact that, overall, they are less likely than men to commit acts of violence or terrorism. To give context to the discussion of women's radicalisation, I consider the roles women have historically played in far-right movements and the precedent of women's participation in radicalised communities. After that, the main part of the book is dedicated to analysing how women are drawn into digital far-right communities via online radicalisation, looking into both the how and the why. The book ends with an exploration of how women are treated in these communities, touching on the misogyny, violence and abuse they are subjected to, before looking to the future and asking what we can do to create a world where this kind of radicalisation is neither possible nor appealing.

We'll meet several of the key players involved in the alt-right movement and in the contemporary far right in the Anglosphere and Europe. This includes men who acted as the architects of the alt-right, such as Richard Spencer, the former journalist who coined the term, Steve Bannon, once editor-in-chief of Breitbart, which was considered to be one of the foremost publications of the alt-right, and later a political strategist in the Trump administration. We'll also discuss the Trump administration and the ways in which it mainstreamed and normalised alt-right political thought, helping to bring it offline and onto the steps of the Capitol Building.

We'll meet women who have acted as propagandists for the alt-right and contemporary far right, including Lauren Southern, the Canadian YouTuber and reporter who is perhaps the best-known female face of the alt-right. There's also Candace Owens, another alt-right political pundit who continues to work for far-right media outlets to this day. We'll also look at the rise of so-called tradwives, short for 'traditional wives', meeting the content creators pushing for a return to regressive Western gender roles where women are financially reliant on their husbands, including Caitlin Huber (better known as Mrs Midwest), one of the most prominent influencers in the tradwife movement, as well as Ayla Stewart (aka Wife with a Purpose), another well-known tradwife content creator. To discuss these, we'll use the term 'far-right female influencers' (FFIs), as proposed by extremism researcher Eviane Leidig in her book *The Women of the Far Right: Social Media Influencers and Online Radicalization.*[13]

While I was writing this book, the digital landscape of tradwives and FFIs has changed significantly. The word 'tradwife' has gone from being one discussed mostly by researchers to an everyday term, thanks to an explosion of media attention in 2023–2024. This media blitz was sparked by interest in a new generation of tradwives, particularly Nara Smith, a model in her own right and the wife of American model Lucky Blue Smith. Smith rose to virality by creating videos in which she'd bake popular processed snacks, such as Oreos or Cookie Crisp cereal, from scratch. Another subject of contemporary media attention is Hannah Neeleman, better known online as 'Ballerina Farms', who posts about her life on a traditional homestead with her husband and eight children. This book does not explore these newer content creators in depth, but instead seeks to provide the context behind tradwives and explain the political roots of the movement, which becomes all the more important as the term broadens and changes in more mainstream usage.

We'll also look at the way in which religious fundamentalism overlaps with both the alt-right and the tradwife movement, and the women who rose to prominence in this sphere, namely sisters Bethany Beal and Kristen Clark, better known as Girl Defined, who make content preaching the value of 'traditional womanhood'.

Moving into the contemporary far right, we'll look at the women who have risen to political power via far-right parties, such as Marine Le Pen, leader of France's National Rally party (previously National Front), who ran for president in 2012, 2017, and 2022. We'll also look at Giorgia Meloni, leader of the Brothers of Italy party and the first female Prime Minister of Italy, whose election campaign focused on traditional family values and emphasised Meloni's role as a mother.

Although less electorally successful, we'll look at contemporary far-right parties in the UK, notably Patriotic Alternative, the largest neo-Nazi group in the country, whose deputy leader, Laura Towler, uses appeals to domesticity and traditional motherhood to recruit new followers. We'll also hear from Lucy Brown, a self-identified 'former' (a term used by people who have left extremist movements), who was once a part of Tommy Robinson's film crew as he toured the country stirring up racial hatred, to hear first hand about the ways in which these movements appeal to, radicalise and ultimately harm women. I met Brown on the hottest day of the year in 2023. During the lift ride up to the conference room where I conducted our interview she complimented my jewellery. Less than two hours later, she told me that Darren Osbourne, who committed a racially aggravated murder in Finsbury Park in 2017, had printouts of Tommy Robinson's – her boss at the time – website in his van. It was a stark reminder of the ways in which white women can use appeals to civility to cover for their dangerous beliefs and rhetoric. Brown was friendly and polite, but she also showed me racist and antisemitic memes on her phone in an attempt to get me to agree with her that they were funny.

In this book, I use 'alt-right' to refer to the far-right movement which existed roughly between the mid-2000s and the mid-2010s, reaching the height of its power and prominence during the Trump presidency (in this book I am only referring to the 2016–2020 Trump administration). It is a movement that existed primarily online, although it made several notable steps offline and had eclectic roots in the manosphere, sceptic, rationalist and new atheist movements, trolling and forum culture, the European new right, identitarianism and several other far-right traditions. The antiracist research group Hope Not Hate summarises it as: 'a far right, antiglobalist grouping that offers a radical "alternative" to traditional/establishment conservatism'.[14]

I use 'far right' as an umbrella term to encompass politics and movements including white nationalism, white supremacy, neo-Nazism, fascism, national conservatism, Evangelicalism, Christo-fascism, populist politics and the alt-right, among others. The European Center for Populism Studies succinctly defines the far right as:

> politics further on the right of the left–right spectrum than the standard political right, particularly in terms of extreme nationalism, nativist ideologies, and authoritarian tendencies. Used to describe the historical experiences of fascism and Nazism, it today includes neo-fascism, neo-Nazism, Third Position, the alt-right, white nationalism and other ideologies or organizations that feature ultranationalist, chauvinist, xenophobic, theocratic, racist, homophobic, anticommunist, or reactionary views.[15]

In this book, I use 'radicalised' or 'radicalisation' colloquially to capture the process of a person's views shifting further and further to the right, outside the Overton window – the window of socially acceptable policies and rhetoric that politicians must stay within in order to retain support and legitimacy, as suggested by American political scientist Joseph Overton – to a point where they encourage, tolerate or even commit acts of violence based on those views. We should be aware, though, that 'radicalisation' is a contentious and political term. Who gets to decide which views are considered 'radical' or 'extremist', as opposed to moderate and acceptable, should be of concern to us all. Many of us who lean left consider the politics of neoliberalism, which condemns countless people to the slow death of poverty, to be an intolerable, extremist act of violence.

Throughout this book, we'll examine the ways in which the alt-right and contemporary far right have successfully shifted the Overton window increasingly rightward.

Lastly, 'fascism' is notoriously controversial and difficult to define, with some scholars and journalists now arguing that the word has become so broad as to have become useless. There have been times in my personal life when I have been guilty of this, defining 'fascist' as whoever happened to be on the other side of a police picket line to me. However, in this book I use it in the way proposed by the Italian novelist and academic Umberto Eco, to describe right-wing authoritarianism in broad strokes, as well as the (inter) personal tendency towards violence, authoritarianism, traditionalism, reactionism and a fear of difference. To quote Paul Mason, 'fascism is a fear of freedom, triggered by a glimpse of freedom'.[16]

1

Girl-fascism defined: understanding the alt-right and far right

The video starts the way most make-up tutorials do: two conventionally attractive blonde women sit facing the camera. The background, which is in soft focus, is a wall lined with inspirational quotes in frames. There's the kind of light, jingly music that you can find on copyright-free sites. It's only when the two sisters start speaking that the video diverges from the norm.

'In this video', explains the slightly older of the two women, who both look to be in their twenties or early thirties, 'we're going to be discussing something fun and practical. How to wear makeup in a God honoring way.'

The video, which has since been deleted from its original channel, was first posted in 2018 and quickly went viral. How could it not? Those of us who didn't grow up in Evangelical communities are always shocked by these little glimpses behind the curtain and this one was prime internet fodder. 'Is this a parody?! This is hilarious!' reads the top comment on the Facebook post sharing the video on the sisters' channel. The video was ridiculed and parodied to within an inch of its life and is still a pop culture touchpoint. Even in 2020, drag queen Trixie Mattel made a video reaction of it, which currently has over four million views. Another reaction video from the channel *That's Cringe* currently has 34 million views. 'How to do [something very unchristian] in a God honoring way' memes still pop up on social media sites regularly, including one of my favourite variations, inspired by lyrics from Megan Thee Stallion's WAP: 'How to be a certified freak, seven days a week, in a God honouring way'.

I first saw the video back in 2018, after someone on my Facebook feed shared it with a jokey caption. Like most people, I found it pretty cringe-worthy and delighted in mocking it, along with several of my friends. But unlike most of my friends, I then followed the video back to the sisters' YouTube channel and fell down a rabbit hole into their brand and blog, Girl Defined. Most of the videos are similar to 'How to wear makeup in a God honoring way'. At first glance, the Girl Defined YouTube channel could be one of the thousands of lifestyle and vlog channels out there. Topics covered include fashion, dating, marriage and social media, all with a Christian twist.

But the more I scrolled and the more I watched, I couldn't help feeling like there was something odd behind the fairy lights and quirky thumbnails. Take, for example, the two-part series entitled 'God's Design for Sexuality', which contains such lines as:

God had a blank slate. He chose to create whatever he wanted. He made a man and a woman. He designed them to be fully sexual. And that's something that I often associate like God and sex, sexuality, like that they go together. Like, he made us this way on purpose. He designed her sexuality. Then he took this man and woman. Put them in a permanent relationship.

And

So when we think about the covenant of marriage, we think, okay, the way that God designed it, it's supposed to be designed. It's supposed to be permanent and it's supposed to be intimate. He created sex to be enjoyed within the context of marriage and that was not an accident.

As a queer person, this set my alarm bells ringing. While on the surface these might seem like statements about faith and sexuality, they are the same biblical arguments used to deny queer people the legal protection of marriage for generations. They subtly testify to a worldview that seeks to restrict reproductive freedoms and demonise any relationships outside those between cis men and women.

As I dug further into the sisters' blog, reaching back through years' worth of archives, their content got increasingly right-wing and bigoted. For example, in a blog published in 2019 entitled 'Same-Sex Attraction and the Christian Girl', the sisters write: 'Sister, regardless of your daily temptation and struggle with same-sex attraction, your temptations are not beyond the reach of God's power. In Him there is true hope, freedom, and new life. Sadly though, the society that we live in will not point you to this awesome Redeemer.' While most of us can identify and even dismiss this as a toxic relic from another, less accepting time, preserved in the amber of Evangelism, scrolling through their blog I came across the kind of hate that can't be glossed over with a sympathetic smile and some nice lighting.

There were several instances of unabashed transphobia, Islamophobia, racism and whorephobia. For example, in a blog post from 2016 entitled 'Thinking Clearly in the Most Dysfunctional GENDERation Ever', they write: 'What if a person despises being male or female, and "invents" a new gender? Would that be okay? What if a 60-year-old woman decides she is actually a 10-year-old little boy in her personal reality? Can she be true to herself? Would surgery be okay? Why wouldn't it be?'

In an article from 2016 entitled 'How to Show Love towards Prostitutes, Homosexuals, and Muslims', one of the pair, Bethany Beal, writes:

> I'll be totally honest with you. In the past (and still at times) I've struggled to view lost people with compassion and love. When I hear the words 'homosexual,' 'prostitute' or even the word 'Muslim' I cringe inside. In my sinful pride I wonder how those people could choose that lifestyle or religion. I think to myself, 'Don't they know how wrong that is?' 'Don't they understand how unfulfilling that is?'

Many of these articles have since been removed from the Girl Defined website, but they are still accessible via the Wayback Machine and other internet archives.

The experience of staring at a ridiculous viral post but quickly finding it led me down a path of bigotry felt oddly familiar. It is a common tactic among the far right, particularly the British far right, as William Allchorn, an expert on radical-right extremist social movements in the UK, notes.[1] Usually, far-right movements will differentiate between the content on their front-facing social media, such as their Facebook, YouTube or Instagram feeds, and their back-facing presence, such as their website or blogs. Generally, content on their front-facing media is more socially acceptable, a milder form of their beliefs, whereas their back-facing media is more directed at their followers or people interested in their movements, as opposed to people who may have just stumbled across it. This content, like that on the Girl Defined blog, tends to be more openly bigoted or extremist – outside of what may be considered socially acceptable.

I had discovered this a few years earlier when a similar process had happened. In my teens and early twenties, I would regularly engage in a sort of emotional self-harm by seeking out content and websites that would cause me emotional distress. This included a lot of homo/biphobic content, but the websites that sucked me in the most were a loose constellation that make up the manosphere. I had first stumbled across them in my early teens after an article called '5 Reasons to Date a Girl with an Eating Disorder' went viral for similar reasons to the Girl Defined video. Once I discovered the manosphere, I kept going back to it, picking at the scab until it bled.

The manosphere consists of websites, blogs and forums from all different breeds of misogynists, including pick-up artists, men going their own way (MGTOW), men's rights activists (MRAs) and incels. Its main trade and export is misogyny and anti-feminism. Pick-up artists, as the name suggests, offer men tips and advice on how to get women into bed. At best, the advice is deeply dependent on regressive gender stereotypes, and at worst, it outright encourages coercive rape and assault. It would be natural to assume that MGTOW were the least dangerous of this community, as their ideology, on the surface, is about male separatism: swearing off intimate relationships and even everyday interactions with women, who they see as being favoured in 'gynocentric' society. But, like the other three core manosphere groups, MGTOW forums and platforms are infested with violent rhetoric and hatred towards women.

MRAs have the most convincing veneer of legitimacy of the manosphere: on the surface, they claim to be interested in addressing issues facing men, with a particular focus on what they see as a biased family court system. However, like the other groups, their real focus is on attacking women's rights and furthering anti-feminism and reactionary misogyny. Hope Not Hate, a charity dedicated to countering extremist messaging, explains that one of the core shared beliefs of the manosphere is that feminism is about misandry rather than women's liberation, meaning that many of its interests and ideas are inherently sexist, anti-feminist and misogynistic, others, such as concerns about male suicide, are not themselves expressions of these. Rather, they are viewed in the manosphere through a lens which places the blame for such issues at the feet of women, feminism and progressive politics.[2]

Incels are the most dangerous subset of the manosphere. Short for 'involuntary celibate', these men blame women for their inability to find sexual partners. Within their insular communities, incels' frustrations fester into a deep and vicious hatred of women, who they see as too shallow and self-absorbed to have sex with men who don't meet the cultural perception of ideal manhood. For them, that means no one other than 'chads' – men with perfect bone structures, ripped bodies, and blessed with being at least 6 feet tall – has a chance of bedding or being loved by women. Their answers to this perceived injustice range from giving up (including committing suicide) to committing femicide as an act of revenge.

Several men radicalised in incel communities have done both, most notably Elliot Rodger, a self-identified incel who killed seven people (including himself) in a misogynistic attack in Isla Vista, California in 2014. Before the spree, Rodger posted a final YouTube video in which he complained about the sexual rejection he had experienced and outlined his plans for the attack.[3] Laura Bates, the author of *Men Who Hate Women*, summarises the incel ideology like this: 'if women's

sexual autonomy has given them wicked and tyrannical control over men's lives, then women's liberation
is at the root of all male suffering. Therefore, the obvious remedy is to remove women's freedom and independence, and to use specifically sexual means (like
rape and sexual slavery) to do so.'[4] She argues that
incels constitute a male supremacist hate group.

The '5 Reasons to Date a Girl with an Eating
Disorder' article was originally posted on one of the
most prominent manosphere sites throughout the
2010s, Return of Kings, which boasted 82,000 unique
users in February of 2016.[5] It was the brainchild of
Daryush Valizadeh, better known by his online moniker Roosh V, who founded the site in 2012, having run
two previous blogs and written several books. Valizadeh
gained notoriety by promoting rape and harassment
under the thin guise of pick-up artistry. The tactics he
preached to his followers included following women
down the street, entering their houses through deceit,
taking advantage of them when drunk and ignoring
their explicit 'no's. 'All pick-up artistry – "game," they
call it – assumes women's boundaries are permeable,
that stalking equals romance and "no" means "try
harder"', writes feminist activist Lindy West, who was
on the receiving end of a particularly vicious harassment campaign initiated by Valizadeh. 'When you see
how rabidly these men rail against the idea of affirma-
tive consent – of obtaining an enthusiastic "yes" rather
than the absence of a no – you realise that a lack of
consent is part of the appeal.'[6]

I visited Return of Kings regularly for a couple of years, between about 2013 and 2015, and in that time I saw it slowly evolve from articles about 'the problems with modern women' and how to 'day game' girls, to why feminists were responsible for the downfall of Western civilisation and refugees from Middle Eastern countries were the reason young men today can't find a good wife. Observing from the sidelines, I watched in slow motion as young men who were looking for ways to get a girlfriend in a very misguided place were spoon-fed a diet of misogyny and other types of bigotry that mutated into overt alt-right and neo-Nazi ideology.

For example, in 2018 they posted a blog called 'How to Overthrow the New Master Race: Western Women', which ended like this:

> When the Islamist or migrant uprising goes into full tilt in the West, refuse to fight it and just let it be. Hostile outside forces are the means to re-masculinizing the West. Use these enemies of your enemy to do your dirty work for you because when it is all said and done, Western men will rise to the top in any male-dominated society.[7]

That's extremely blatant Western supremacy. By the time these ideas had spread from some kooky corner of the internet that no one took seriously to become mainstream talking points buoyed up by the 2016 election, I was already well acquainted with most of the major players from the manosphere. This included Milo Yiannopoulos, a British far-right political commentator,

Jordan Peterson, a Canadian psychologist and perhaps one of the best-known names of the 'intellectual dark web', Paul Elam, founder of prominent men's rights website A Voice For Men, and even Steve Bannon. These men became the face of the alt-right in its heyday, changing the shape of public discourse and opinion on a global scale. They even became familiar figures in the White House under Trump's administration. I watched as they lured in sad, lonely boys on janky blogs about picking up women, and spat out angry, violent men.

A lot of time, attention and research has gone into understanding how the internet has been used as one of the most effective tools in the far-right armoury for recruiting young men. But for nearly a decade, as I watched neo-Nazis with tiki torches march through Portland, white supremacists attack Black churches, extremists drive into crowds of protesters and Trump supporters storm the Capitol Building of the United States, and even as I faced off against Tommy Robinson supporters in the streets of London, I kept noticing the presence of a demographic that surely couldn't have got its start in the misogynist cesspit of the manosphere.

And I couldn't help but think back to those Girl Defined videos, with their bigotry dolled up in fairy lights and tips on hosting the best dinner party.

How many women are in the far right?

In 2016, 47 per cent of white women voted for Donald Trump, compared to 45 per cent who voted for Hillary

Clinton, according to the Pew Research Center.[8] As journalist Molly Ball noted in *Time* magazine, 'that's still a plurality, and still makes white women more Trump-positive than the overall electorate, which supported Clinton by a 48%–46% margin'.[9] Then, in 2020, 52 per cent of white women voted for him, according to the same study. For comparison, 94 per cent of Black women, 67 per cent of Hispanic women and 72 per cent of Asian women voted for Biden. White men voted for Trump by a majority of 58 per cent.[10]

Given his overt sexism and how damaging for women his four-year term was, why did so many white women vote for him? When you look at previous elections, it's not actually that surprising. In fact, white women supported previous Republican candidates, including Romney, Bush and Reagan, by even bigger margins. Feminist journalist Moira Donegan suggests that the intersection of white women's race and gender places them in a 'curious position', where they have structural power thanks to their race yet are excluded from it on the basis of sex. She writes:

> In a political system where racism and sexism are both so deeply ingrained, white women must choose to be loyal to either the more powerful aspect of their identity, their race, or to the less powerful, their sex. Some Republican white women might lean into racism not only for racism's sake, but also as a means of avoiding or denying the realities of how sexist oppression makes them vulnerable.[11]

But just because millions of white women were willing to vote for an authoritarian populist in spite of the threat he posed to their rights and liberties doesn't necessarily make them all alt-right radicals, right?

Many were lifelong Republican voters, Evangelicals and paleo-conservatives who voted in loyalty to their religion, their economic interests and their traditionalism. Many will have voted simply in step with their husbands. These factors, too, point to a wider discussion about women's role in furthering right-wing politics and white supremacy, one that cannot be easily captured by who voted for Trump and who voted for Clinton. In addition, as many BIPOC (Black, Indigenous, People of Colour) feminists and writers argued at the time, while Hillary Clinton's campaign was progressive in comparison to Trump's, she was still running on a ticket that upheld imperialism, sidelined (at best) issues that affected women of colour and represented a type of corporate feminism that has now come to be known as 'Girlboss', 'Lean In' (after the book by former Facebook COO Sheryl Sandberg) or white feminism.

Zillah Eisenstein, an American political theorist and gender studies scholar who called the 2016 election 'the election from hell, between a misogynist racist bigot and an imperial feminist', wrote at the time that Clinton

disguises militarism with a friendly white female face, read as feminist, as though this feminism were inclusive when it is not. When a woman is president, we – women – will be told that the glass ceiling has been broken. We will hear that we are now in a post-feminist era. But this particular 'we' remains too rich, too white, too imperial, too capitalist, too everything that most women (and men) are not.[12]

Among some of the left and liberals, arguments about Clinton's credentials as a feminist or what her presidency might mean for women and minorities were sometimes met with the accusation that not voting for Clinton or even publicly criticising her was aiding the alt-right.

In order to better explore this, let's first unpack what the alt-right is, its origins and how it differs from other far-right and hard-right movements.

Short for 'alternative right', the term alt-right was coined by white supremacist Richard Spencer in an article he wrote for the far-right publication *Taki's Magazine* in 2008. In the article, Spencer used the term to distinguish a group of people on the right who differed from establishment conservatives (at the time) by opposing egalitarianism, multiculturalism and open immigration, among other things. The Southern Poverty Law Center (SPLC), meanwhile, describes the alt-right as 'a set of far-right ideologies, groups and individuals whose core belief is that 'white identity' is under attack by multicultural forces using 'political correctness' and 'social justice' to undermine white people and 'their' civilization'.[13]

The alt-right gained popularity steadily between 2010 and 2015 and entered mainstream consciousness during the 2016 election, when Donald Trump hired Steve Bannon, co-founder of Breitbart News, one of the key media outlets of the alt-right, as his chief strategist.[14] The movement was at its strongest during Trump's four-year presidency. Buoyed up by (often cryptic) support from the president, it spread rapidly online and took several violent steps into the real world. The most notable were the Unite the Right rally of 2017, which ended with multiple injuries and the death of counter-protester Heather Hayer, and 6 January 2021 insurrection, in which protesters stormed the Capitol Building in Washington, DC, directly resulting in the death of Ashli Babbitt (although several other protesters and one police officer died in the days following, their deaths have since been attributed underlying health conditions and drug use).[15] The movement lost momentum and support rapidly after the Capitol attack, and the loss of mainstream political support via the end of the Trump presidency choked what remained of much of its oxygen supply.[16] Some left the movement, some stayed where they were as their views became more mainstream, and many moved further right into extremist groups or conspiracy communities such as QAnon.

There are several subgroups within the alt-right, such as identitarians, radical traditionals, and the Proud Boys, but the overarching ideology is the same: the superiority of white people as well as the general inferiority of women. In a policy paper for the International Center for Counter-Terrorism, researchers Tore Bjørgo and

Jacob Aasland Ravndal explain that both the alt-right and Identitarian movement fall within ethnonationalism, the European identitarians focus more on cultural nationalism, whereas the American alt-right gravitate more towards racial nationalism. Antisemitism and Islamophobia are also core tenets of the movement, leading many people to argue that the alt-right is just neo-Nazism in a nicer suit. As the Anti-Defamation League (ADL) notes,

> Alt righters use terms like 'culture' as substitutes for more divisive terms such as 'race,' and promote 'Western Civilization' as a code word for white culture or identity. They tend to avoid explicit white supremacist references like the '14 words,' a slogan used by neo-Nazis and other hardcore white supremacists. While alt-righters share the sentiment behind the '14 words' they're more inclined to talk about preserving European-American identity.[17]

Others see the alt-right as an iteration of white nationalism. 'Their commitment to white supremacy is what makes them white nationalists, denizens of the far right, supporters of the hate movement', explains Seyward Darby in her book *Sisters in Hate: American Women on the Front Lines of White Nationalism*.[18] Yet others argue that the alt-right is the moderate fringe of the far right and functions as a gateway to more radical movements. 'The alt-right, in my opinion, they're a facet of the far-right, but they're like the weed. That's the so-called gateway drug, and then the neo-Nazi[s are] the heroin', journalist Jake Hanrahan, who spent several years investigating Atomwaffen and several other neo-Nazi groups, explained to me in 2020.

While some writers, particularly journalists reporting at the time, have used the terms 'alt-right' and 'far right' interchangeably, Hanrahan believes it is important to make a distinction between the two, as these movements define themselves by and are specific in their use of this terminology and which groups they identify with. He explains that much of the alt-right tried to deny or obfuscate its extremism, arguing that they were just trying to bring conservatism back into the mainstream (some may even believe this). In contrast, he says, neo-Nazis are open about their violent intentions towards marginalised groups such as queer people, Jewish people and people of colour. Being aware of these distinctions has become more important as the alt-right dissolves and its denizens disperse into other, in some cases more extreme, movements.

There is truth to all of these theories. The alt-right is not a monolith and it being inextricable and opaque to outsiders is deliberate. This is partly to create a feeling of 'insider' status for members through a shared sociolect and visual language. It also allows members plausible deniability and distance from the more extremist views and politics, as well as allowing the alt-right to 'Hide [its] Power Level', a phrase borrowed from the anime *Dragon Ball Z*, to mean cloaking the movement's size and strength. Finally, it reflects the alt-right's roots in, and overlap with, online troll communities. The alt-right aims to recruit and tends to be made up of young, college-educated, white men. It is heavily influenced by online culture. The use of memes, messaging boards and so-called ironic humour are the key ways this ideology spreads.[19]

In 2016, the Institute for Family Studies (IFS) suggested that about 6 per cent of Americans agreed with the three core beliefs of the alt-right, which they identified as: (1) a strong sense of white identity, (2) a belief in the importance of white solidarity and (3) a sense of white victimisation.[20] Similarly, in 2017 a survey suggested that about 10 per cent of Americans identified with the alt-right. (It should be noted that the IFS is an explicitly religious and conservative organisation, dedicated to promoting traditional marriage and family values. This research into the alt-right aimed to disprove that being religious and married were key indicators of whether someone held alt-right views.) That might not sound like much, but given that America has a population of about 328.2 million, that's still around 32.82 million people.

As we can see, the alt-right is pretty sizeable, and any sizeable movement will inevitably have women in it, regardless of how openly misogynistic it is. In an interview that took place on the day of the Capitol riots, Daniel Lombroso, who spent four years researching the alt-right, told me that he believes that at the time women made up roughly one in ten of the attendees he would see at the average alt-right conference. 'The easiest example I can think of was the first conference I covered. Richard Spencer threw basically a coming-out party for President Trump when he won. At that conference, there were about 250 people. I think maybe 10 to 20 percent were women', he said.

As well as this anecdotal evidence, the IFS also found that women were more likely to agree with the three core beliefs than their male counterparts. According to their research, 5.99 per cent of American women agreed with the three core tenets of the alt-right, compared to 5.24 per cent of American men. More recently, Hilary Matfess and Devorah Margolin, researchers for the Program on Extremism at George Washington University, found that 102 women participated in the 6 January riot, in comparison to 664 men.[21] 'There's always a presence, and they like to pride themselves on saying that there are women, this isn't purely a male movement', explains Daniel Lombroso. He believes that women are not only tokenised within the alt-right to make it seem more respectable but have also 'absorbed so much anti-feminism that they really believe that they have a duty in this movement. It's a duty that the men spell out and even the women spell out very clearly, which is that they're supposed to be baby-makers.' As we'll explore later, women played a pivotal organisational role in the riot.

The alt-right, far right and other white supremacists believe that white people will eventually be overtaken in numbers by non-white people (including Jewish people) and that they have a duty to protect the white race and white cultures. This is known as 'Great Replacement theory' and has its roots in the antisemitic conspiracy theory 'the protocols of the elders of Zion', which posits that Jewish leaders are engineering the decline in white birth rates. Hence Proud Boys notoriously led a chant of 'Jews will not replace us' at the Unite the Right rally. In order to not be replaced, white supremacist movements need white babies, and they cannot have white babies without cis white women and announced female at birth people (including forcibly detransitioned transmasc and certain non-binary people). While these movements are aware of this and many seek to recruit white cis women into the role of 'birthers of the nation', it's also important to note at this stage that women's *willingness* to produce white babies for the movement is considered tangential at best: far-right and white supremacist movements are almost always aligned with forced-birth (while they refer to themselves as 'pro-life', this book uses the term 'forced birth' to better represent the intent of such policies) advocates.

Women's role in the alt-right

It may seem contradictory for women to align themselves with a movement that seeks ultimately to restrict their autonomy and reproductive rights, but the narrative of pro-natalism is what appeals to many women who join these groups. Seyward Darby notes that, 'for white nationalism as a movement, a big theme is women's intrinsic value as wives and mothers. For women who might be seeking a sense of meaning or a degree of power they don't have, this is a movement that says we value you in terms of how you look and who you are and what your body enables you to do.'[22] Natalist narratives put women in positions of power in which they are gatekeepers of the race; objects deserving of reverence and protection based on what their body can (hypothetically) do. Although, as we will explore later, this position of power does not often play out in reality.

However, women aren't just passive baby makers and housewives within these groups – they're also recruitment tools and powerful propagandists. Their presence adds a veneer of legitimacy and respectability to these hate movements, as well as making them seem more approachable and welcoming compared to the feeling created by aggressive male leaders. This is nothing new. As I show in Chapter 2, women have been used as the smiling faces of far-right movements throughout history.

2

Forward to the past: the history of women in far-right movements

Look at any hate group throughout history and you'll find women. From the Ku Klux Klan (KKK) to the National Socialist Women's League to Women for Trump, women have buoyed the ranks of far-right and white supremacist movements from their inception, sometimes stepping into the spotlight and sometimes lurking in the shadows.

Women have played varied roles in these communities, and while they have not, generally speaking, committed violence with their own hands, as this chapter explores, they have often shaped, directed and partaken in the violence committed by their male allies. The history of women in far-right movements is often obscured or erased, but women's involvement has been indispensable at all stages, from formation to expansion, normalisation and bloodshed. While many men in the far right may deny it, and many women may try to overlook it, the truth is that at every level and every step of the process, women's labour has been crucial. In this chapter I take a closer look at some of the most notable women who have helped to shape the far right throughout history.

Savitri Devi: Hitler's priestess

Women have helped to shape the thought architecture of fascism and its modern offshoots, including conspiracy-based movements such as QAnon. Savitri Devi, born Maximiani Portas, a Greek national who adopted Hinduism, was one of the key influences behind the neo-Nazi and far-right fascination with mysticism. Known as 'Hitler's Priestess', Devi was inspired by Hindu nationalism, as well as ancient Egyptian religions, and dedicated much of her adult life to 'find[ing] spiritual roots for national socialism'.[1] She believed in Indigenous Aryanism, a conspiracy theory that the Aryan race originated from the subcontinent of India, and the Indo-European languages and people then dispersed outwards across Europe. She felt that India represented the best of racial segregation and sought to export its caste system as a model of racial suppression.[2]

During the Second World War, Devi gathered intelligence for the Axis alongside her husband, Asit Krishna Mukherji, an editor of the pro-German newspaper *New Mercury*. After the war, she travelled around Europe, visiting places she considered Nazi sacred sites and preaching Nazism as a spirituality. 'In her wide-ranging spiritual doctrine', writes Alexander Reid Ross, 'Devi tied together a collection of scriptures in order to find the revealed knowledge of white supremacist power that could regenerate Nazism'.[3] She went on to propagandise for the return of the Nazis, travelling from country to country, including India and Spain. During this time, Devi became part of a 'tight-knit circle of fascist organisers' and one of the preeminent spiritual leaders of neofascism.

Throughout the 1960s and 1970s, Devi continued to promote neo-Nazism and Holocaust denial. She corresponded with neo-Nazi organisations all over the world, including the World Union of National Socialists, the British National Party (BNP), the National Front and the American Nazi Party. After her death in 1982, her ashes were interred at the headquarters of the American Nazi Party in Arlington, Virginia, next to those of its founder, George Lincoln Rockwell. Devi's spiritual influence on neo-Nazism and the wider far-right and white supremacist movement can still be felt today, from its links to Hindu nationalism and esoteric justifications for Aryan superiority to the use of new-age and wellness communities as recruiting grounds. Devi helped to shape much of the 'feminine mysticism' that permeates both far-right and conspiracy spaces and is often interwoven in far-right women.

Elizabeth Tyler: propagandist for the KKK

As well as contributing to fascist beliefs, women acting as propagandists for far-right hate movements also has a deep historical precedent. In *The Second Coming of the KKK*, historian Linda Gordon points out that women were instrumental in the resurgence of the Klan in the early 1900s, with several taking on leadership and propagandist positions, despite the organisation's supposed adherence to traditional gender roles. One key example is Elizabeth Tyler, a widow who remarried into the Klan. Tyler had an affair with Edward Clarke, who was hired alongside her to run the organisation's PR firm and newspaper, *Searchlight*.

The couple were arrested in 1919, when their extramarital activities were discovered. Clarke resigned from the group during their hearings but Tyler refused. She even used the publicity to drum up more interest in the KKK. As Gordon writes, 'Tyler was finally forced to resign by accusations, almost certainly true, of embezzling Klan money. But she had been a gift to the national Klan. The organisation might well have grown without this driven, bold, corrupt, and precariously entrepreneurial woman, but it would likely have been smaller.'[4] One of Tyler's most enduring legacies was expanding the KKK's list of enemies to include communists, Jewish people and immigrants, among others, in order to appeal to a broader base. She also cloaked the KKK's white supremacy in the language of social welfare, 'a move that would become a hallmark of the modern-day right', as the journalist Laura Smith has suggested.[5]

Elizabeth Tyler is just one of the numerous white women who took on roles as preachers and organisers within the second incarnation of the KKK. In fact, Gordon claims that one in six Klan members were women. That amounts to between half a million and three million participants of the hate group, which was responsible for atrocities – including lynchings – against

Black communities. Women organised so-called family-friendly Klan events such as picnics, sewed robes and handled administrative duties. As Smith warns, it's important not to downplay women's power within the Klan; though they were 'staunch defenders of traditional domesticity, they were also active in social welfare movements and local and state politics', she notes.[6]

The women's branch of the Klan (WKKK) lobbied for the creation of racist immigration quotas, segregation and anti-miscegenation laws. Daisy Barr, co-found of the WKKK, pushed the mythos that the KKK and white supremacy were bastions of white women's protection and interests. In doing so, she linked white women's empowerment and family values with white supremacy and nationalism. 'The cross burnings and eerie robes of the Klan were the most sensational expression of the terror group's strategy, but likely not its most effective', Smith writes. 'The blending of racism with more wholesome causes – security, family life, and patriotism – may be white supremacy's darkest and most enduring legacy.'[7]

While men in the KKK may have gotten their hands dirty by committing direct violence, women were often instigators. Protecting white women from the sexualised threat of Black men was a core aim of the Klan, and white women did not shy away from the power their tears and finger-pointing gave them. Ida B. Wells, an anti-lynching campaigner, posited that lynchings were not a form of mob justice for sexual violence or encroaching on white women's decency but a mechanism of white supremacist terror.[8] Taken in this light, false accusations made by white women against Black men could be seen as stochastic terrorism – that is, making statements that implicitly advocate for violence without directly calling for it. White women in the modern far-right and white nationalist movements have continued to exploit this power, urging men to step up to protect them from the threat posed by immigrant men or men of colour.

Rotha Lintorn-Orman: mother of British fascism

Women's role in the history of the far right and white supremacy is not limited to one side of the Atlantic. In the UK, women have been central to the British fascist movement throughout its history. Sprouting in the interwar period, British fascism blended the ideology of Italian fascism with British nationalism. Several factions emerged, including Oswald Mosley's British Union of Fascists, the Imperial Fascist League and the New Party. But the first explicitly fascist group in the UK was the British Fascists, also known by the Italicised name British Fascisti.

The British Fascisti was founded by a woman, Rotha Lintorn-Orman, in 1923 in reaction to the news that the Labour Party had sent a delegation to a Socialist Party conference in Hamburg. Lintorn-Orman came from an ultranationalist background and saw the idea of fascism as a way of fighting back against the increasing power of the left. Although the party was her brainchild, she was not at its helm. 'She was originally just the founder because there was a definite incongruity between women's leadership and a fascist movement. Fascist movements are by their very definition masculine-oriented, even male-supremacist', explained Julie Gottlieb, author of *Feminine Fascism: Women in Britain's Fascist Movement, 1923–1945*, to me in an interview over Zoom in 2020.

The party collapsed in 1934, but the legacy of British fascism continued, reaching its peak with the British Union of Fascists (BUF). While the BUF was, like all fascist movements, inherently hyper-masculine and male supremacist, Mosley's party appealed to and recruited women as a way to secure and expand its membership base. The party's support of (white British) women's rights proved popular, with women eventually constituting up to 15 per cent of the membership. 'In that sense, the British Union of Fascists advocated many policies that were feminist by the standards of their own day', explains Gottlieb. This included equal pay for equal work and the abolition of the marriage bar. But the party's support of women's rights 'served as a double-edged sword': on the one hand it gave them cover to claim to be less misogynistic than they were, which helped them appeal to female voters. On the other, it allowed them to placate men in the movement by suggesting that giving women equal pay meant they wouldn't push men out of the labour market.

The BUF was not unique among fascist movements in trying to play both hands in this way. Both the interwar Italian fascist movement and the Nazi Party managed to appeal to both men and women by seeming to align themselves with women's interests while allaying men's anxiety about women's role in the labour market following their return from the front lines in the First World War. They did so by offering a sense of power to women via participation in the party, while implementing policies that effectively drove them back into the domestic sphere, and in doing so created less competition for men in the labour market.[9]

Like other fascist movements before it, the BUF even appealed to some feminist groups, notably the Suffragettes. Three prominent Suffragettes, Mary Richardson, Norah Elam and Mary Allen, moved from one group to the other. This made sense in many ways, as women could be active and effective participants in the BUF. 'As doorstep canvassers, the women presented a more reassuring image of fascism than that created by street violence and mass demonstrations', writes historian Martin Pugh, whose work focuses on women's social and political history in the nineteenth and twentieth century.[10] Beyond providing a softer face for fascism, as well as reproductive labour, women in the BUF trained in jiu-jitsu alongside male Blackshirts, as it was considered more appropriate for them to manhandle female communists and anti-fascists who disrupted their rallies and meetings.

The move made sense ideologically too. During the First World War, some of the Suffragettes took a staunchly patriotic position (although the organisation's official stance was that of pacifism), and outside of their progressive aim for (white) women's suffrage, several of the founders and organiser held much more conservative views. 'In some sense, the ex-suffragette fascists still regarded themselves as feminists', continues Pugh. 'However, they had become detached from the feminist movement which, like most fascists, they regarded as a symptom of a degraded political system.'[11]

This strain of British white feminism can still be seen today in the modern far-right and the gender critical movements, which grew out of the trans(gender) exclusionary radical feminist (TERF) movement, and rejects the notion of gender in its entirety, claiming that women are solely oppressed on the basis of sex and that it is impossible for a person to transition from one sex to another. In a (now deleted) article for *Vice*, journalist Vic Parsons explains that the term 'gender critical' is closely associated with the 'anti-gender' movement of the far and religious right. They quote the Black feminist writer Lola Olufemi, who says that '[t]his is not a coincidence. Their understanding of sex and gender as fixed, "biological" facts is fascistic in that fact seeks to impose a "right" order on human populations.' Olufemi goes on to assert that, unlike grassroots feminism, gender critical feminism embodies neoliberalism in its focus on law, legislation and the rights of the individual citizen.[12]

Alison Phipps, author of *Me Not You: The Trouble with Mainstream Feminism*, refers to this as the 'fascistic habit' of white feminism and white womanhood; the tendency to struggle for white women's empowerment at the expense of other marginalised people, whether it's women of colour, immigrants or queer people.[13] Let's not forget that many suffragists in the US campaigned for white women's right to vote by arguing it would reduce the power of Black men, who had recently been granted the vote themselves (although barriers to citizenship – necessary for voting – still existed in several states). As Koa Beck, author of *White Feminism*, notes: 'In 1893 [the National American Woman Suffrage Association] had passed a resolution under President Susan B. Anthony that thinly pledged middle- and upper-class white women's allegiance to white capitalism if they were to get the right to vote.'[14] Is it really a surprise that many of the women whose fight for their own suffrage was rooted in nationalism crossed into fascist parties once that aim had been achieved?

Marine Le Pen: taking fascism mainstream

Women have been indispensable in modern fascism too, playing a significant role in the rising tide of far-right ideologies and populism across Europe over the last decade. At the time of writing, several countries in Europe have far-right governments, including Hungary, Italy and the Netherlands. Other European countries, including Austria, Germany and France, have increasingly popular far-right parties, while several of those parties, including Italy's, France's and Denmark's, are led by women.

The increasing number of women in leadership roles may be thanks to the example set in France by Marine Le Pen, leader of the anti-immigration party National Rally, previously known as National Front. Marine is the daughter of National Rally founder Jean-Marie Le Pen, a convicted racist and Holocaust denier. After becoming president of the party in 2012, Le Pen stated that her aim was the 'de-demonisation' and softening of the party's image.

In 2017, Le Pen ran for president of France on a platform of anti-immigration, economic nationalism and protectionism, France's withdrawal from the EU, anti-globalism – including withdrawing from NATO – anti-multiculturalism and unabashed Islamophobia. She has a history of implying that most Muslims are extremists and, following a terrorist attack in 2017, she called for the closure of all 'extremist' mosques, insinuating that meant all or at least most of them. Despite this, her presidential campaign emphasised Le Pen as a softer, more feminine figure than her father. She went on to win 34 per cent of the vote, less than the polls had predicted but still over a third of those cast. In 2020, she won 41.5 per cent of votes in the presidential election against Emmanuel Macron.[15]

In June 2024, while I was writing this book, Macron dissolved the National Assembly and called a snap election. He was motivated by recent losses in the European Parliament, which had seen Le Pen's party win 31 per cent of the vote, double that of Macron's Renaissance party.[16] Despite fears and predictions of a National Rally victory – which would have meant France had a far-right government for the first time since the Second World War[17] – the party was defeated by the leftist coalition the New Popular Front, which won the most seats (188), followed by Emmanuel Macron's centrist Ensemble coalition (161 seats). National Rally came third, securing 142 seats.[18]

Jayda Fransen: twenty-first-century fascist

In the UK, one of the more influential women in the modern far right is Jayda Fransen, who cut her teeth in the English Defence League (EDL) before becoming deputy leader of the British fascist political group Britain First in 2014. She acted as the group's temporary leader for six months in 2016, after actual leader Paul Golding was arrested for breaching a court order banning him from entering a mosque or encouraging others to do so.

Britain First was founded in 2011 by former members of the BNP. The BNP is regarded as a neo-Nazi organisation, promoting at various points in its history the forced removal of non-white citizens from the UK, racial segregation, an end to interracial unions, Holocaust denial and Islamophobia. Unlike the BNP, the EDL is not a formal political party; having grown out of football hooliganism, the group regularly engaged in street brawls with anti-fascists. There is significant overlap in the EDL's, BNP's and Britain First's membership and followers. Fransen regularly appeared on what was left of the EDL's social media pages as the organisation fizzled out of existence. Hope Not Hate notes that while the BNP emerged from an adherence to Nazism, and the EDL is 'a tabloid headline-driven car-crash of alcoholic misspent patriotism and violent criminality and Islamophobia', Britain First's leadership is driven by a man dedicated to 'Calvinist chauvinism, religious bigotry and the raptures of evangelical and biblical Armageddon prophecies'.[19]

Fransen, and Britain First in general, are best known for their so-called Christian patrols, in which they would march through predominantly Muslim areas carrying white crosses and a banner reading 'We Are the British Resistance', pouring beer on the ground outside of mosques. They also broadcast footage of themselves entering mosques to hand out bibles and leaflets on so-called Muslim grooming gangs on social media. In 2017, Trump retweeted three videos posted by Fransen which she claimed showed Muslims committing violence against non-Muslims. All three videos have been debunked.

While Fransen is now much less active in the British far right, her participation in these groups demonstrates how women have played important roles in every iteration of the far-right movement, from organised political parties to street mobs. She was perhaps one of the earliest FFIs, using social media in its earlier days to spread Britain First's message, along with videos of their actions, bridging the gap between the digital far right and real-world violence.

As these examples show, there's plenty of precedent for women playing active roles in far-right groups throughout history, despite or even because of those groups' regressive views on gender. This raises the question of why women's active participation in modern far-right groups, including the alt-right, is treated as such a novelty. As journalists Claire Provost and Lara Whyte write for OpenDemocracy: 'Women are more active and visible in political life all over the world; perhaps it is not surprising at all that they are also represented in these movements too. The idea that women are naturally "peaceful," or less likely to espouse hateful or divisive views, is also an unhelpful stereotype.'[20]

Perhaps the general erasure of women from history is also to blame for our amnesia over women's roles in some of the most atrocious moments from our past. Perhaps the 'benevolent' sexist view that sees women as caring and motherly by nature has also shielded us, especially those of us who are white, from being seen as capable of acts of hatred and violence. In *Sisters in Hate*, Seyward Darby chalks this up to the 'women are wonderful effect', noting that 'the savviest white nationalists are aware of the blind spot that observers often have when it comes to women, discounting their contributions to abhorrent causes because they prefer to think of them as humanity's better angels'.[21]

But Julie Gottlieb disagrees. She believes that the opposite may be true and that women in far-right movements have been glamorised and sexualised. 'I think we have given a lot of attention to fascist women because it's a sexy subject', she explained to me in our interview. 'We have these two seemingly incongruous elements of women and fascism, and when we bring them together, we figure there'll be fireworks.' She went on to say that while many still make the initial assumption that the far right is male-dominated and male-led, there is a growing field of study dedicated to understanding women in the far right. It is to this field that this book hopes to contribute.

Now that we understand that women have always been present and played key roles in white supremacist and far-right movements, it is less surprising that they do so in the modern, post-internet, far-right. But given how misogynistic these movements are, and how prominent a role anti-feminism has played in the radicalisation of men, how have women been drawn in, and how have they risen through the ranks? What can the political evolution of women such as Lauren Southern, Laura Lokteff and Candace Owens, three of the most well-known figures in the alt-right, teach us about the radicalisation of women and the threat posed by it? To understand this, we first need to understand what the far right believes about women and their role in the world.

3

This is what they took from you: the far right's vision for women

To the far right, women exist only as commodities. Their commodification is manifold. Women are sexual objects. Women are sources of domestic and reproductive labour. And, like land to be conquered, women are symbols of men's virility and power. All far-right movements are male supremacist, but the alt-right is perhaps most prominent in explicitly using anti-feminism and misogyny in its core recruitment tactics and focusing on a return to gender hierarchy as one of the main goals of the movement.

The Institute for Research on Male Supremacism (IRMS) defines male supremacy as 'a cultural, political, economic, and social system, in which cisgender men disproportionately control status, power, and resources, and women, trans men, and non-binary people are subordinated'.[1] As Alex DiBranco, co-founder of the IRMS, explained to me over Zoom: 'It's founded on a deep biological gender essentialism. So anything also that violates the concept of a gender order around two sexes is something that male supremacism attacks.' This chapter explores how the alt-right's formation in the manosphere shaped its gender politics and what this can show us about women's radicalisation into the contemporary far right.

First, we should cover the term 'gender ideology', which is used by the far right to demonise issues that primarily (or traditionally) affect anyone who isn't a cisgender, heterosexual man, or anything which is seen as challenging the nuclear family (and its place as the centre of our lives under capitalism). This includes topics such as queer rights, abortion, childcare, feminism and sex workers' rights. In her book *Bodies under Siege*, investigative journalist Sian Norris argues that fascist ideology consists of three core tenets: (1) the belief that progress is subverting the natural order, (2) the belief that to return to the natural order we must revert to a pre-Enlightenment state where 'nature rather than reason dictates human behavior' and (3) that human nature is inherently violent and therefore a constant state of war is natural.[2] It is the first two tenets that reveal how the far right conceptualises women: to fascists, the natural order is a hierarchy wherein women are subservient to men, people of colour are inferior to white people, and queer people don't exist at all (as queerness is seen as being 'unnatural'). The third, as we will see throughout this chapter, is used to justify the inferiority and domination of women, who, in the fascist mind, are physically weaker and therefore more vulnerable than men.

'Gender ideology', then, is anything that is seen as progressing away from the so-called natural order.

The anti-gender backlash began in earnest among right-wing Catholic groups as early as 1994, after the term was inscribed in intergovernmental documentation for the first time at the Cairo International Conference on Population and Development. Six months later, at the Preparatory Committee Meeting for the IV World Conference on Women, the concept was openly attacked by US Catholic groups.[3] Since then, the anti-gender-ideology crusade has become one of the most ferocious and arguably successful taken up by the post-war right.

Over two decades later, in 2018, Hungary's far-right Prime Minister, Viktor Orbán, revoked accreditation and funding for gender studies programmes in universities across the country (only two universities offered courses at the time). 'The government's standpoint is that people are born either male or female, and we do not consider it acceptable for us to talk about socially constructed genders rather than biological sexes', a spokesman for the Prime Minister said of the decision.[4] Arguably, this move was a watershed for attacks on trans and queer rights within EU countries. The emptiness and elasticity of the phrase 'gender ideology' means it can be evoked as a bogeyman in any number of contexts and for any number of ends. Sonia Corrêa, the director of Sexual Policy Watch in Brazil, writes that 'anti-gender proponents mobilise simplistic logics and imaginaries and constitute volatile enemies – here the feminists, there the gays, over there the artists, ahead the academics, elsewhere the trans bodies – nourishing moral panics that distract societies from structural issues that they should be debating, such as growing inequalities of gender, class, race and ethnicity'.[5] This demonstrates how the versatility of the gender ideologies concept allows it to be weaponised against any group considered undesirable, no matter how tenuous the connection.

To the far right, gender is synonymous with women and with deviation from the default, which is to say men and masculinity. Masculinity is the core of fascist regimes. It is strength, discipline, violence and virility. Women, and gender as a construct, represent weakness: chaos, nurturing and fertility. As with wider society, the sexism of the far right ranges from ambivalent, to benevolent, to hostile. Gender and gender ideology is also seen as linked to both Jewishness and Communism in the eyes of the far right, and both women's rights and queer rights issues are often demonised as 'cultural Marxist' conspiracies. 'The phrase refers to a kind of "political correctness" on steroids – a covert assault on the American way of life that allegedly has been developed by the left over the course of the last 70 years', explains the SPLC.[6]

Gamergate and the anti-feminism of the alt-right

To understand how the anti-gender backlash of the alt-right became so successful, you first have to understand Gamergate and the ambient sexism of internet culture in the mid-2010s. Four years before Orbán's ban, video game developer Eron Gjoni posted a 9,425-word blog falsely accusing his ex-girlfriend, Zoe Quinn, of sleeping with a journalist in exchange for positive reviews of her indie game (the reviews in question never actually materialised).[7] Gjoni and Quinn had met less than a year before. Having connected on OkCupid, they dated for just five months. A few months after their breakup, they slept together again at a games conference in San Francisco, where Quinn was speaking on a panel, after Gjoni had sent a lengthy email begging to get back together and accusing her of cheating on him during their courtship (which she denied). Quinn alleges that Gjoni turned violent during their final encounter, leaving bruises on her arms. Gjoni denies the allegation. After the encounter he spent months emailing, texting and messaging her, before writing and publishing 'The Zoe Post'. Gjoni published the post on multiple websites, including Something Awful, a web 1.0-style forum similar to 4chan in both its audience and the type of content it houses, and a dedicated WordPress blog, which is still active as of writing.

The reaction to 'The Zoe Post' snowballed into months of targeted harassment against several prominent women involved in gaming. At its core, Gamergate was a right-wing, reactionary backlash against feminism's growing influence on gaming culture. It was also a tale as old as time: an angry ex-boyfriend stalking a woman who'd spurned him and moved on. 'It is domestic abuse that went viral, and it was designed to go viral', Quinn told *Boston Magazine* in 2015. But this time, Gjoni had a new weapon at his fingertips: the internet and masses of men hungry for blood. Today, we might refer to Gjoni's behaviour as cyberstalking or digital harassment. But in 2014, when 'The Zoe Post' was unleashed on the world, social media was in its adolescence and still considered a novelty, and laws to protect people from the real-life harms it could inflict were still in their infancy. The judge who granted Quinn's restraining order stumbled over the terminology for what Gjoni had done.[8]

It's no coincidence that Gamergate unfolded while the manosphere was at its peak. The culture of the internet helped Gamergate grow into the harassment campaign it became, and from there into a proto-culture war. Expanding on previous work by Fred Turner and Lori Kendall, researchers Sarah Banet-Weiser and Kate M. Miltner have explored how the foundations of the social web were created largely by white, male users originating in the scientific and military industrial complex of the mid-twentieth century. 'In these cultures', they write, 'aggression was accepted (if not standard) and Habermasian rational-critical speech was privileged'. Noting that some scholars have theorised that a lack of visual and social cues in early web forums was to blame for the 'rampant antagonism' within those communities, Banet-Weiser and Miltner go on to argue that 'these normative structures continue to operate in primarily white, male-dominated "geek" spaces'.[9]

That is to say, while the hegemony of white supremacy and patriarchy are often thought of and presented as products of human nature or as having evolved on their own, they are in fact the product of white men's creation. This is because white men are considered the default against which all others are measured. So, while we may think of the culture of the internet as global and egalitarian, it is perhaps much more influenced by its origins, including its origins as a military tool.

As several academics and organisations have noted, the manosphere played a key role in the radicalisation of young men into the alt-right and far right. In 2019, UK anti-extremism charity Hope Not Hate included the mansosphere in their 'State of Hate' report for the first time, noting that:

> The prevailing interpretation within the manosphere is that feminism is about promoting misandry (contempt or prejudice of men) rather than gender equality. [...] The manosphere's core ideas have snowballed into an ideology that has taken on a life of its own outside of its online niche, in part because the rejection of feminism and a broader conspiratorial outlook continues to find resonance with the wider contemporary far right.[10]

Perhaps ironically, a big accelerant in the pipeline from the manosphere to the alt-right was a website and community known as PUAhate.com. While this might sound like a website dedicated to rallying against those who've gamified human intimacy and deeply warped the way many young men view women, it was actually a space for men who were frustrated with pick-up artistry because of their lack of 'success'. Much of the site's content and discussion blamed women for their sexual failures and inadequacy. You may recognise the name PUAhate.com from being name-checked in the manifesto of the Santa Barbara murderer, Elliot Rodger. In May 2014, Rodger killed six people and injured 14 in a spree-killing motivated by male supremacists and incel ideology. While Rodger was not the first incel murderer, he was arguably the one who catapulted the ideology to mainstream media attention. From there, many other copycats followed in his footsteps, often trying to beat his 'high score' (body count), and in doing so cause as much backlash and reaction as possible. Here, we can see the gamification of pick-up artist spaces reflected in the violence they provoke.

The gamification of violence fits into a tactic used by the far right known as 'accelerationism'. Zack Beauchamp, a senior correspondent at *Vox*, has called accelerationism 'one of the dominant ideas on the fringe right'.[11] The term originated in Marxism but was later picked up and warped by far-right philosopher Nick Land. Accelerationists aim to speed up the degradation and collapse of society in order to usher in revolution, or in the case of white nationalists/supremacists, civil/race war (respectively). '[V]iolent far-right extremists' adoption of it as a strategy is relatively recent', writes Cynthia Miller-Idriss, a sociologist and head of the Polarization & Extremism Research & Innovation Lab (PERIL). '[It] reflects a major shift from the realm of apocalyptic fantasies into direct action, through a celebration of violence that will bring about an end-times collapse and subsequent restoration of a new white civilization.'[12] Mass murderers other than incels use this tactic, including Dylann Roof, who spoke about wanting to cause a race war by inflaming tensions through his killings. Roof murdered nine Black people as they worshipped in their church in southern California one Wednesday in 2015.

How the alt-right's misogyny differs from other far-right movements

What do the alt-right's roots in the manosphere mean for women in the movement? While historic and party/organisation-based movements such as those touched upon in Chapter 2 were male supremacist, the alt-right is distinguished by its use of anti-feminism as a core radicalisation tactic. To learn more, I spoke to Eviane Leidig, author of the book *The Women of the Far-Right: Social Media Influencers and Online Radicalization*. 'It is important to stress that the "alt-right" is just one of many contemporary far-right movements', she told me, before going on to explain:

> The label 'alt-right' was deliberately used by leaders and supporters as a sanitising term to create a favourable public image, despite building off a longer legacy of hate movements. The alt-right's views on gender and sexuality are not so different from other far-right movements. Traditional notions of femininity and masculinity as tied to biological (and racial) reproduction is the guiding norm.

Much of the movement's overarching politics is about restoring traditional gender roles and dynamics between (cisgender heterosexual) men and women. This is done (with significant success, as we discuss later) by spreading online propaganda about what women's lives should look like via memes, forums, videos, podcasts, streams and influencers. Yet women play crucial roles within these communities, often in ways that seem to contradict what they themselves are saying.

The far right has always viewed women as subservient, although the patriarchal utopia they desire differs between factions. For the alt-right, this looks like a 'return' to the perceived gender norms of the middle of the twentieth century, where men are the sole breadwinners and women are confined to the domestic sphere. In this vision, women are chaste, feminine, ever-smiling mothers whose singular purpose is to serve their husband and family – in that order. This vision of postwar domesticity is both exclusionary and ahistorical. It belongs to what the philosopher Jason Stanley, author of *How Fascism Works*, calls the 'mythic past' of fascism, an imagined glorious era in which everything was uniform and in keeping with the natural order.[13] This mythic past is characterised by nostalgia for an imagined time before a country had not yet been ruined by cosmopolitan elites and progressives, including feminists and migrants, and racial purity was the norm – enshrined via the domination of women. Such an era is often referred to by fascist groups themselves as a 'simpler time'.

Yet their envisioned domestic sphere, bedecked with gingham and white goods, was mostly the domain of white, middle-class women, whose husbands could afford to support them through their (often unionised) salaried jobs. And even within the white middle classes, women's return to the home after the war was not ubiquitous. Despite societal norms that encouraged women to stay in the home and out of the workplace, partly in order to free up jobs for returning servicemen, approximately 40 per cent of women with young children, and at least half of women with older children, chose to remain in the workforce.[14]

This image of idealised postwar womanhood and nuclear family life arose in part due to the Cold War. It served to link 'traditional' (although at the time fairly novel) gender roles to national security and in opposition to the threat of Communism. Communism itself is viewed by the far right as being inherently Jewish (which is a pejorative in their worldview), meaning its challenge to this idealised American version of womanhood is simultaneously a threat to capitalism and Christianity – since Communism overthrowing capitalism would also result in Judaism succeeding Christianity as the dominant religion of the West.

Feminism, particularly second-wave feminism, which began in the 1960s with a focus on liberating women from the shackles of domesticity, is often described similarly within the far right as 'cultural Marxism' or a 'cultural Marxist plot'. Cultural Marxism is sometimes cited on the far right as being the brainchild of a small group of Jewish philosophers who, after fleeing Germany, devised a new form of Marxism which focused on America's culture, as opposed to its economic system.[15] Thus, the alt-right links women's obedience and a return to perceived pre-second-wave feminist domesticity with a return to national and racial greatness.

The view that we need to return to a world where women are just homemakers and babymakers is known as the 'tradwife' movement and is popular with both men and women. In her article 'Red Pill Factories', Jessica Stern, a research professor at Boston University's Pardee School of Global Studies, lays out the core idea:

> Trad Wives believe the heterosexual world to be a marketplace, where women are the sellers and men the buyers of sex. A woman's sexual market value, or SMV, is a measure of her appeal to men. Only appearances matter: a sense of humour, an education or exotic interests are irrelevant.[16]

Tradwives, like the alt-right, believe women exist to serve men. Women are seen as biologically weaker, less intelligent and more emotionally unstable. Because of this, many in the alt-right and the tradwife communities believe women should not work but rather spend their time 'barefoot and pregnant' in the home. Others go as far as arguing that women should not have the right to vote or own property. 'When you give a female choice of which political leader to vote into office, who do they vote for? The one who is more handsome and promises unsustainable freebies that accelerate the decline of her country', Roosh V once wrote for the popular manosphere website Return of Kings.[17] He went on to propose that every woman should be under the guardianship of a man, from whom she would need to get approval on everything from her sexual partners to her diet and clothes. In this dystopian vision, women would not have their own money, be able to get a degree (except, he generously noted, in exceptional circumstances) or participate in democracy. To begin with, this guardian would be her father or a male relative, until she was married, wherein her ownership would be transferred to her husband.

Meet the tradwives

Why would women embrace an ideology that seeks to limit their autonomy, including their bodily autonomy, much less evangelise for it? The reasons are as multifaceted as the women themselves, but many feel betrayed by modernity and see the tradwife role as an empowering alternative. 'We shouldn't underestimate how some young white women, when faced with this bleak economic landscape and then presented with a rosy image of 1950s domestic bliss, may look back to 1960s Friedan-era feminism as having cheated them out of a family and a luxurious lifestyle', writes far-right and anti-feminism researcher Annie Kelly. 'The men on the alt-right might point to diversity initiatives and mass immigration as having dismantled their career prospects; the women are furious that they have to consider career prospects at all.'[18]

A TikTok by content creator Jennifer Mock (99,800 followers as of February 2023) illustrates this type of thinking perfectly. In it, Mock plays both a demure, apron-wearing 1950s housewife and an obnoxious, purple-haired modern woman. Her modern-day alter-ego welcomes the housewife to the future by telling her she 'can do anything a man can do'. After being told she no longer has to wear an apron, the housewife asks, 'do we finally have a butler to cook for us?' The modern woman explains no, she'll eat processed food and still have to clean the house after work, but can have as much casual sex as she wants thanks to the birth control pill and freely available abortions. The housewife, disgusted, asks if she will at least be happy. The 'punchline' of the video is the modern woman saying 'yes, as long as you don't skip your antidepressant pill'. The video has 374,000 likes at the time of writing, though since posting it Mock has made her account private.

It's interesting to note that Mock's housewife's (and by implication her own) view of liberated simplicity relies on the existence of an exploited class who would provide domestic labour instead of women. Another example comes from the Telegram channel Fascinating Womanhood (3,792 subscribers as of August 2024), which posted on 29 November 2022 that '[t]he feminist agenda says that it's perfectly normal to clean, teach and take care of lots of children, cook or bake for hours in a kitchen, and submit to the authority of men. Just as long as it's not your own home, your own children, your own kitchen, or your own husband.' Here again, we can see some of the frustration at liberal feminism, where women are still responsible for reproductive labour, yet the criticism places the blame on the desire for women's liberation itself, as opposed to the failings of capitalist feminism. This argument creates a false dichotomy wherein women's only options are working outside the home while also shouldering the majority of domestic and reproductive labour, or giving up waged work in favour of being a stay-at-home wife/girlfriend/mother.

This of course ignores the many ways in which women have fought for liberation, including the Wages for Housework movement, which tried to make visible just how reliant the capitalist economy is on the free or underpaid labour of women within the household. 'Social perceptions have also consistently failed to value housework', writes Yanitra Kumaraguru, a lecturer in law at the University of Colombo, 'both in terms of its contribution to the family and to the larger economy, despite the contribution made by women in the form of unpaid care and domestic work being estimated at as much as nine percent of the global GDP [gross domestic product] in recent years'.[19] While the Wages for Housework movement has become less relevant recently, it provides a framework with which to push back against the argument made by tradwives that only a return to traditional gender roles can liberate women from the expectation that they must continue to fulfil all the domestic chores and child-rearing necessary to maintaining a household and family, on top of performing paid labour outside the home.

Some women feel duped by the promises of the sexual revolution and see the landscape of contemporary dating and hook-up culture as unequal or even degrading for women. '[T]he sexual revolution turned everything on its head and somehow painted traditional courtship as misogynistic and offensive to women because our sexuality is not something to be bought or even earned', writes Gina Florio in the right-wing *Evie Magazine*. 'Sex soon became free and easy to achieve, and this was all wrapped up in a fake little bow of empowerment and feminism. But this comes at a price.' As she goes on to say:

> We don't need peer-reviewed studies or scientific data to tell us that random sex is unnatural and detrimental. As much as we try to deny our nature and demand that we can 'have sex like a man,' there's something that happens all the way down to our soul when we give our body away for free to any guy that we find mildly attractive.[20]

This grievance about the sexual revolution is not entirely unfounded; while the loosening of cultural mores (as well as the creation of dating apps) has made casual sex more accessible and acceptable for both men and women (and people outside of that binary), this has not necessarily made heterosexual relationships/ encounters more equitable or fulfilling for women.

'In a context of already destigmatized and open hetero-sexual expression, sex-positive thinking could begin to look like a mandate towards women's sexual avail-ability; not a defence of women's sexual freedom but a reassertion of men's sexual entitlement', writes femi-nist journalist Moira Donegan.[21] Nor has the rise in hook-up culture been coupled with an increase in cis men's respect for or sense of responsibility towards cis women's sexual needs (including that of negating unwanted pregnancies). This latter point came to a head in June 2022, when *Roe v. Wade* was overturned in America and 'trigger bans' were activated in almost half the country, leaving millions without access to legal abortion almost overnight.

The tradwife movement isn't strictly alt-right. It doesn't necessarily have a political position, other than advocating for a return to so-called traditional Western gender roles. A lot of the tradwife move-ment overlaps with the fundamental Christian right, which is where Bethany Beal and Kristen Clark of Girl Defined would most likely fall on the political spectrum. The modern Christian right movement was started by the televangelist Jerry Falwell in the 1960s, when he mobilised white Christians to oppose desegregating schools.[22] Since then, it has fought back against any kind of progress in regard to human rights, including same-sex marriage and better access to abortion, by claiming that they infringe on religious liberties. As Sarah Posner, author of *Unholy: How White Christian Nationalists Powered the Trump*

Presidency, and the Devastating Legacy They Left Behind, explains:

> [T]oday, Trump's base echoes similar claims of perse-cution – claiming that LGBTQ+ rights, for example, infringe on Christians' religious freedom, or that state governors' restrictions on large gatherings during the COVID-19 pandemic infringe on the first amendment rights of churches. Throughout his candidacy and pres-idency, white Evangelicals have stood behind Trump because, many of them say, he is 'the most pro-religious freedom' president in history.[23]

In general, there's a lot of overlap of groups within the far right, with many of them having similar ideologies and visions, albeit with different plans regarding how to achieve them. In this way, Girl Defined's teach-ings of 'biblical femininity', in which they encour-age women to act as a 'helpmate' for their husband, finds purchase with tradwives, including those who may not consider themselves Evangelical. 'Why you should embrace the lost art of homemaking', reads the opening slide of a beige Instagram carousel on Girl Defined's grid. Reasons include 'hospitality is com-manded' and 'order and peace in a chaotic world'. The post was liked by several tradwife accounts. Many so-called tradwife influencers are Evangelical Christians or Mormons, and while most have right-wing or even far-right beliefs, their accounts tend to focus on pro-moting traditional/biblical womanhood as opposed to sharing overtly political content (not that gender isn't political).

Here, we must acknowledge the spectrum of public tradwives: from those whose focus is purely on gender and how it is expected to be expressed, to those of the alt-right, where sharing tradwife content is intended to further an agenda that aims at establishing an ethno-state. (I personally refer to the latter as the 'RETVRN tradwives', in reference to the memes that are nostalgic for the fascist mythic past often shared across far-right online communities. In these memes, 'RETURN' is often stylised as 'RETVRN', perhaps in reference to classic Latin.) Sophia Sykes and Veronica Hopner of Massey University in Aotearoa, New Zealand see the 'tradwife landscape' as spanning three categories of content creators. Ranging from least to most extreme, these are: conservative tradwives, alt-lite tradwives and alt-right tradwives. Across this landscape, Sykes and Hopner identify four subcategories (Figure 3.1): conservative (which spans all three categories); political (conservative right and alt-lite tradwives); militia tradwives; and counterculture tradwives (both alt-lite and alt-right tradwives).[24]

As Sykes and Hopner explain:

Conservative Right tradwives advocate for a #Tradlife within the home, supporting their husbands and children. These tradwives had clear conservative values on politics and religion but, on the whole, did not overtly engage with issues of race. Conversely, Alt-Right tradwives were less characterised by the traditional housewife framing and instead presented an ideological online persona rooted in Alt-Right identities which enshrined value systems such as white supremacy,

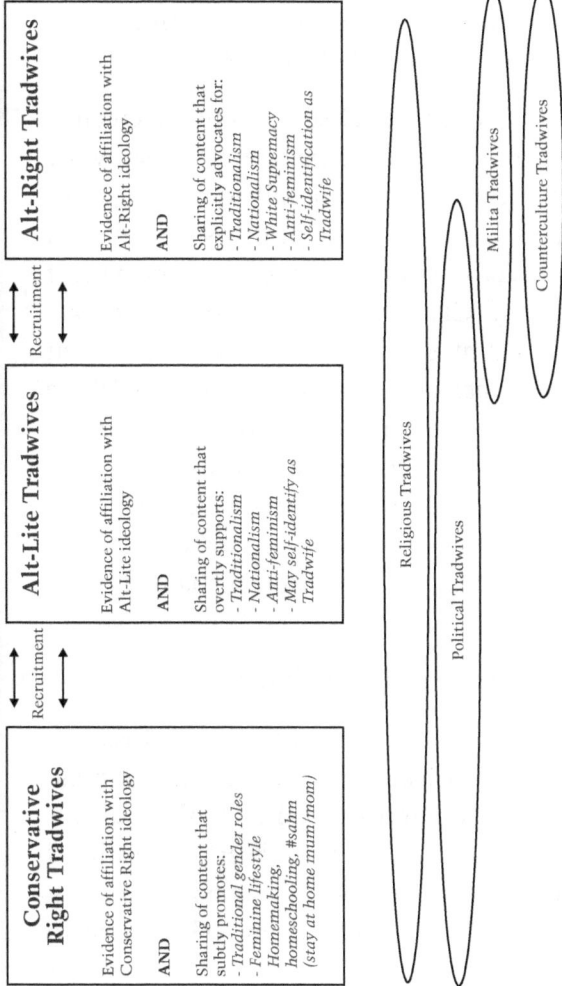

Conservative Right Tradwives		**Alt-Lite Tradwives**		**Alt-Right Tradwives**
Evidence of affiliation with Conservative Right ideology	*Recruitment*	Evidence of affiliation with Alt-Lite ideology	*Recruitment*	Evidence of affiliation with Alt-Right ideology
AND		**AND**		**AND**
Sharing of content that subtly promotes: - *Traditional gender roles* - *Feminine lifestyle* - *Homemaking,* *homeschooling, #sahm* *(stay at home mum/mom)*		Sharing of content that overtly supports: - *Traditionalism* - *Nationalism* - *Anti-feminism* - *May self-identify as* *Tradwife*		Sharing of content that explicitly advocates for: - *Traditionalism* - *Nationalism* - *White Supremacy* - *Anti-feminism* - *Self-identification as* *Tradwife*

Religious Tradwives

Political Tradwives

Milita Tradwives

Counterculture Tradwives

Least extreme   Most extreme

Figure 3.1 The tradwife landscape

Source: Sophia Sykes. 'Tradwives: The Housewives Commodifying Right-Wing Ideology'. GNET, 7 July 2023, http://gnet-research.org/2023/07/07/tradwives-the-housewives-commodifying-right-wing-ideology/. Accessed 4 July 2024.

heteropatriarchy, and anti-feminism. Alt-lite tradwives were the bridge between Conservative Right and Alt-Right women, presenting a blended balance between the traditional feminine persona of Conservative trad-wives, and the ideologically driven Alt-Right.[25]

In their research, which tracked 36 content creators across ten months, Sykes and Hopner found that while ideological affiliation was not mutually exclusive, most tradwife content creators tend to prioritise one type of expression in order to curate their online persona. For example, Beal and Clark fall into the religious trad-wife category, and most likely the conservative right to possibly alt-lite part of the tradwife spectrum. While they promote heteropatriarchal ideals, they rarely if ever mention race within their social feeds or content. In fact, unlike alt-lite to alt-right tradwives, there are sometimes religious women of colour featured on the Girl Defined Instagram and other social channels.

Tradwives and the alt-right

While the tradwife movement stretches across the spectrum of the political right, it was at its most notable – and found the most support – within the alt-right, whose views on gender were best encapsulated by it. Women are objectified, not just as sexual objects, but as a pillar of Western civilisation. They need to be protected by men but also to act as a reward for those men for upholding Western society. Dr Ashley Mattheis, whose research focuses on digital cultures of the far right, refers to this as 'the ultimate romantic gesture'[26] that men in the far right offer women: saving Western civilisation for them. In return, white women must be worth fighting for.

'I think the message to these men [of the alt-right] is that if you join our movement, you'll find other women like us', Eviane Leidig explained to me in an interview over Zoom. 'So it's sort of like the potential that they tried to offer. In many ways, these women are seen to legitimise or to normalise far-right narratives and ideologies, which are quite harmful.' She went on to explain that women are considered less 'boisterous and aggressive', meaning they provide a more welcoming face to those exploring far-right ideologies than militant, male-dominant groups such as the Proud Boys. In this way, the role of women is twofold. First, they act to legitimise these groups through their mere presence by reassuring outsiders that these movements aren't just a violent boy's clubs. Second, they provide an incentive for male recruits, by presenting them with something 'worth fighting for'. This refrain is popular across the far-right digisphere. It is the name of a well-known Instagram account and clothing brand. The account worth_fighting_for on Instagram currently has 165,000 followers. The majority of the imagery on the account consists of collages, often of women in traditional European dress, 1950s Americana or comparisons of 'modern culture', such as women in suits, brutalist architecture or other representations of cultural degeneration contrasted with thatched dwellings, families and modest women, intended to represent the fascist mythic past and the idealised vision for white womanhood.

This is a common theme among the memes and images shared on far-right channels. Images often include drawings of smiling white families, in stereotypical 1950s attire, attending church or doing other traditional activities such as having BBQs and walking through cornfields together. These images sometimes have a filter over them to make the post look like it's glitching, with phrases like 'this is what they took from you' or 'forward to the past'. It's also what we see in the original 'wojak' memes of the strong-jawed man and his concerned-looking wife in a floral dress. These images are typical on accounts like worth_fighting_for and trad_wins (both of which seem to exist to promote the clothing brand Worth Fighting For). They are also circulated in private social media spaces (known as 'dark socials'), for example Telegram channels such as White Lad Aesthetic and Traditional Femininity, which share dozens of these images a day, seemingly with the intention of disseminating them across Instagram, Twitter and other public-facing accounts. This shared visual language helps spread the far-right gender ideology memetically.

'The goal of having a woman in the movement is to show an avatar of traditional femininity', journalist Daniel Lombroso explains to me:

> So [they] can say, we have strong men, we have warriors, but we also have these perfect women who fulfil the Aryan ideal. Of course, they're not saying Aryan.

They're saying Western or other euphemisms. But everything from the iconography of the blonde hair and blue eyes, to the words they're using about baby-making harkens back to the traditional role of women in the fascist movements of the twentieth century.

Lombroso spent four years reporting on the alt-right, including creating a documentary about the alt-right's poster girl, Lauren Southern. He likens Southern to a modern-day Phyllis Schlafly, in that she embodies the contradictions of being a mouthpiece for a movement that believes women shouldn't have a voice. Schlafly was a conservative and anti-feminist activist who in the 1970s campaigned against the Equal Rights Amendment, which would have constitutionalised the prohibition of sex-based discrimination. Lombroso notes that both Southern and Schlafly use their platforms to publicly decry feminism and promote traditional gender roles wherein a woman is confined to the home raising children. The irony of this, of course, is that both women stepped outside of their vision of womanhood in order to evangelise it. Further, while Southern spoke of the importance of white women bearing as many white children as possible in order to fight back against 'white genocide' and 'replacement', at the height of her fame as an influencer she was unmarried and childless. Eventually, Southern received so much backlash for not being a mother by her early twenties that she eventually stepped back from the limelight to, in her words, focus on becoming a wife and mother. However, in early 2022, she returned to public life.

Women and the contemporary far right

Despite their very real and violent hatred for women, the far right knows that it needs cis, white women to continue the white race. After all, there can be no increase in white babies without white cis women (and closeted or forcibly detransitioned transmasculine/non-binary people). Many of the female influencers of the alt-right and far right have built their platform around encouraging white women to have as many babies as possible. Most notable for this is Ayla Stewart, known online as Wife with a Purpose, who earned a brief moment of mainstream recognition in 2017 after proposing a 'White Baby Challenge'. 'As a mother of 6, I challenge families to have as many white babies as I have contributed', Stewart tweeted. This is in keeping with women's role in the far right as 'birthers of the nation' or mothers of the nation.

Motherhood is key to both how the far right appeals to women and what it expects of women. Mothers are venerated as warriors, protectors and even goddess-like, and in order to encourage motherhood from its women, the far right uses better support for mothers as a recruitment tactic. 'The same motive led fascists to uphold women's role as the mothers of a reborn and regenerated race, which meant trying to arrest the falling birth rate by means of maternity classes, more female doctors, better paid midwives, more maternity beds and home helps for recuperating mothers', writes historian Martin Pugh, explaining why so many

Suffragettes went on to join fascist movements.[27] More recently, the far-right Alternative for Germany party has attempted to appeal to women on the basis of motherhood in their election manifesto, by promising reforms allowing mothers to be paid €25,000 in child allowance.[28]

Women's role as 'reproductive' labour isn't restricted to their wombs or their own homes. Having a class of subservient labourers is also important for the reproduction of the movement itself. 'Women are always vital to right-wing movements because they provide a labour and organising apparatus. In patriarchal movements, in which women are not expected to work outside of the home, they have a huge population of volunteer labour [from women]', Alex DiBranco, the co-founder and executive director of the IRMS, explains to me over Zoom. Just as Klan robes did not sew themselves, flyers do not print themselves, food for conferences does not order itself and buses to demonstrations do not book themselves. Women act as domestic and reproductive labour not just for their husbands within the movement but for the movement *itself*.

It was the group Women for America First that secured the permit for the Stop the Steal rally, which allowed insurrections to be on the grass outside the Capitol Building on 6 January 2021. 'While militia irregulars, Proud Boys, and other angry white males were plotting on Parler, obtaining military cosplay, and arming themselves with bats and flagpole battering rams in December and early January', notes political journalist Nina Burleigh, 'top-level Trumpist women in Washington power suits were arranging park permits and lining up a large stage and three Jumbotrons, all in the name of women.'[29] Now, groups such as Moms for Liberty (MFL) are collectivising their roles as mothers and housewives to overrun parent teacher association meetings in the name of banning books that contain LGBTQ+ or critical race theory themes. This can be seen as a kind of fun-house mirror reflection of the housewife boycotts Koa Beck outlines in her book *White Feminism*, as a common tactic among immigrant and Jewish housewives for affecting change in their local communities.

The SPLC describes MFL as a far-right organisation that self-identifies as part of the modern parental rights movement and engages in anti-student inclusion. 'The group grew out of opposition to public health regulations for COVID-19, opposes LGBTQ+ and racially inclusive school curriculum, and has advocated books bans', they write, going on to note that MFL goes about this in part by encouraging members to gain positions on local school boards. Within two years of inception, they reported having 250 chapters in 42 states.[30]

'When was the last time you went to your local school board? Maybe it is time to go', suggested MFL in their Telegram channel on 31 August 2023, under a video of a man reading from Jay Asher's suicide-themed young adult novel *Thirteen Reasons Why*. Pen America found '2,532 instances of individual books being banned, affecting 1,648 unique book titles between 2021 and

2022, with 41 per cent of unique titles banned containing LGBTQ+ themes and 40% containing primary or secondary characters of colour'.[31] It's important not to dismiss MFL as just a group of concerned housewives and mothers turning up at meetings. First, that diminishes the importance of feminised labour. Second, MFL is an organised and dedicated fascist group; they may not be stockpiling arms, but they are still causing harm and spreading bigotry, and they are hiding behind our own, internalised misogyny – that women's work is less important and that mothers are an apolitical force for good – to do so.

Gender essentialism and the far right

The alt-right and far right's regressive view of gender relies on essentialism to explain the inalienable differences between men and women. That is, they do not see the difference between men's and women's roles in society as constructed culturally but as a reflection of biological differences between (cis) male and female bodies. Often this is via biological essentialism, examples of which can be seen in a blog post by the popular right-wing author Jordan Peterson called 'The Gender Scandal'. He writes:

> Where are the largest differences? Men are less agreeable (more competitive, harsher, tough-minded, skeptical, unsympathetic, critically-minded, independent, stubborn). This is in keeping with their proclivity, also documented cross-culturally, to manifest higher rates

of violence and antisocial or criminal behavior, such that incarceration rates for men vs women approximate 15:1. Women are higher in negative emotion, or neuroticism. They experience more anxiety, emotional pain, frustration, grief, self-conscious doubt and disappointment (something in keeping with their proclivity to experience depression at twice the rate of men). These differences appear to emerge at puberty. Perhaps it's a consequence of women's smaller size, and the danger that poses in conflict. Perhaps it's a consequence of their sexual vulnerability. Perhaps (and this is the explanation I favor) it's because women have always taken primary care of infants, who are exceptionally vulnerable, and must therefore suffer from hypervigilance to threat.[32]

In this dense paragraph, we can see how Peterson's essentialist attitudes to sex and gender have been spun into an evolutionary worldview used to explain women's oppression via feminised and reproductive labour as part of the natural order: the fascist mythic past to which we must return in order to save Western civilisation.

For other factions of the far right, gender differences are explained by mystic essentialism. That is, the difference between men and women and their roles are ingrained not in social conditioning, or even biology, but in the intelligent design of our possible makers. For Christian right figures such as Girl Defined, this of course means the biblical God. But another strong through line in far-right propaganda and ideology is the Nordic pagan concept of 'the mother and the hunter', or what philosopher Tracy Llanera calls the 'goddess/ victim' archetype of womanhood.[33]

Pagan, particularly Nordic, mysticism is very popular within the far right. It takes many forms, from
the Thulean paganism of the Nazis themselves to the
esoteric Hitlerism of Savitri Devi's neo-Nazism and
the Odinism (*Wotansvolk*) of the white supremacist
terror cell The Order. New-age beliefs provide an alternative framework to justify categorisation and hierarchies. Phil Jones, of the progressive research group
Autonomy, describes far-right occultism as 'merely
the path to ethnonationalist superiority, cosmic violence to earthly tradition'.[34] As with Devi's mysticism,
pagan and new-age beliefs serve to link the far right
to wellness and conspiracy-minded spirituality movements (sometimes referred to with the term 'conspirituality') in a way that appeals to far-right womanhood.
After all, in fascist thought architecture, the mystic
is characterised as feminine, in contrast to masculine
order and rationality.

The term conspirituality, a portmanteau of 'conspiracy theory' and 'spirituality', was coined by anthropol-
ogists Charlotte Ward and David Voas, who summarise
it as 'a broad politico-spiritual philosophy based on
two core convictions, the first traditional to conspiracy
theory, the second rooted in the new age: 1) a secret
group covertly controls, or is trying to control, the
political and social order, and 2) humanity is undergo-
ing a "paradigm shift" in consciousness'.[35]

There are also factions who simply do not give reasons for these differences between genders, beyond
it being 'common sense' or 'just the way things are'.

The ideology and worldview of the far right is often illogical and contradictory and consists of whatever is most useful to defend their preconceived beliefs and desires in the moment. While a better understanding their ideology allows us to better counter them, to pretend the far right always has a consistent ideology is to give them credit where it is often undue.

As well as gender roles, tradwives and the alt-right see women's attractiveness through an essentialist lens, in that they perceive it as inherent. These groups see women's worth as their so-called SMV, which is almost entirely determined by looks. Although these can be slightly enhanced by being thin and feminine, it's mostly dictated by genetic make-up. While it cannot easily be increased, a woman's SMV (and worth) can be depleted by doing things such as cutting their hair short, getting tattoos and piercings, being competitive, having a high-powered career, getting old, refusing to be submissive to men and sleeping around.

Both men and women of the alt-right, far right and manosphere view relationships and dating as a marketplace, where, as the radicalisation researcher Julia Ebner explains in her book *Going Dark: The Secret Lives of Extremists*, 'women are sellers and men buyers of sex'.[36] In this way, women become gatekeepers of a commodity that men desire, and women must therefore be conquered in order to access it. Here, again, we see the men of the far right taking on the role of warrior and invader. In their day-to-day lives, they may be frustrated to the point of despair at their lack of power in their jobs or society at large – what sociologist Michael Kimmel calls 'aggrieved entitlement'[37] – but within the realm of the far right, they are fighting a sacred war to save Western society and the white race from immigrants and declining birth rates.

Women become another obstacle in their way and must give over access to their reproductive capabilities and sexuality either through persuasion or force. This framing also gives (cis, white) women a sense of power they may be lacking in their lives. They are the gatekeepers of the future of the white race, a prize to be fought for and won. 'This radically simplistic view of gender relations is used to legitimise the objectification of women', says Ebner, 'to make it acceptable, even necessary, to rate, trade and replace women – like market goods'. Ebner, who spent months observing communities of tradwife and red pill women, was repeatedly told that '[w]omen's highest value to men is her sexual value, and she's most valuable when she's in her sexually pristine state'.[38]

It must be stressed, though, that while this view of heterosexuality does appeal to some women, it is mostly propagated by the men of the alt-right and far right. If a woman is a thing to be acquired and conquered, her consent is a nicety rather than a necessity. '[I]t's OUR WOMB – that's right, it doesn't belong to her, it belongs to the males in her society – that is being used to produce an enemy soldier', wrote editor Andrew Anglin in a post on the neo-Nazi website *The Daily Stormer* in 2016. One thing that frustrates me about much of the writing around how women are treated within the far right, and how pervasive sexual and domestic violence is, is the way it's seen by many writers and researchers as an unfortunate by-product of a hateful ideology rather than a central mechanism of the system. Far-right communities can purge themselves of ethnic minorities, queer people and anyone else they see as undesirable but, despite their violent hatred of them, they cannot purge themselves of women if they wish to sustain their community and achieve their ethnonationalist ends. The domination of 'good' women, even within these communities, through sexualised violence is central to the movement.

Essentialism, whether biological or mystical, is also how the alt-right and far right view other aspects of identity, especially race. By making these characteristics immutable, they can use them to create hierarchies. 'If one race is superior, another race must be inferior', the feminist writer and campaigner Jane Fae explained to me in an interview in 2020. 'If one race is inferior, it cannot have the same amount of rights. What is going on with the far right, is almost a rejection of universality when it comes to rights, a rejection of the idea of rights as inalienable.' As with gender roles, though, it should be noted that a cohesive ideology is not always necessary for the alt-right and far right to justify their white supremacy or ethnonationalism.

Women's role as the wife and mother to be protected is often weaponised to enforce these racial and ethnic hierarchies, among others. The sociologist Sara R. Farris refers to this as 'femonationalism',[39] where the protection of white women (and white woman-hood) is invoked to demonise men of colour or male immigrants/refugees. In the UK and Europe, anti-immigrant and Islamophobic rhetoric are core tenets around which both the digital far right and party-based far-right groups organise. Muslim men and male migrants are positioned as invaders, coming to the UK and Europe not only to take over the land and over-power Western culture but also to rape and brutalise white women and girls. In the UK, the case of so-called Muslim grooming gangs is often used in far-right prop-aganda and even acted as the catalyst for the emer-gence of new far-right groups. For example, much of EDL founder Tommy Robinson's notoriety came from his arrest for contempt of court, after he livestreamed outside the trial of several men connected with the so-called grooming gangs. He pointed to this as evi-dence of a deep-state conspiracy to cover up the trial and silence anyone 'raising awareness' of its occur-rence. The EDL itself, where Robinson's activism was incubated, 'came into existence rather haphazardly, as a response to a radical Islamist group protesting a procession for returning soldiers', as Sam Moore and Alex Roberts, hosts of the *12 Rules for WHAT* podcast, explain in their book *Post-Internet Far Right: Fascism in the Age of the Internet*.[40]

Positioning white men as the protectors of white women is a powerful tactic for radicalisation. The

Commission for Countering Extremism says that some groups 'deliberately distort the truth to persuade their audience to adopt discriminatory and hateful attitudes' and warned that the tactic was drawing in white communities who would not normally support the far right.[41] Further, in Europe and the UK, Islamophobia is mainstream enough to provide a gateway into more radical ideas while also offering plausible deniability that these views are not extremist or even outside of the norm. 'Those who publicly limit their racism to Muslims, bemoan the supposed suppression of their rights and freedoms and claim to represent the oppressed "people" versus a corrupt "elite" echo the views of much larger sections of the British public and thus have found success in attracting larger numbers than at any time since the 1930s', notes journalist Lizzie Dearden.[42]

Men of the alt-right and far right do not see women as in need of protection from the misogynistic violence of the patriarchy, or even as people deserving of dignity and safety. After all, though it's often represented as a frenzied attack or a loss of control, sexual violence is almost mundane in how it is used to enforce existing power dynamics. The majority of sexual violence is committed by someone the victim knows, usually a partner or family member. Women of colour and other marginalised women, including disabled women[43] and queer women,[44] are at higher risk of experiencing sexual violence. But the far right is not concerned with the reality of sexual violence, or even with protecting white women from it. Rather, this line of thinking is an extension of the far right's aim to preserve racial purity. Women are to be defended not for their own protection but as a commodity to be hoarded and guarded, like land or wealth.

'This faux-concern rooted in a toxic mix of misogyny and ethnonationalism', writes journalist Eleanor Penny, 'gives us a peek into the warped far-right world picture which considers women and girls to be exactly that: land, territory, and property to be defended by force. In other words, sexual violence against women and girls is not considered bad because it's a horrifying violent act, a system of global domination. It's bad only because it's an infringement of white men's property rights.'[45] Rape and other forms of sexual violence are not seen as wrong because of the lasting mental and physical damage they cause but because they are a threat to white women's innocence and purity; in short, they are a threat to the foundation of one's whiteness.

Perhaps this is why some white women rub shoulders with men who use rape as a tool for control and submission while simultaneously expecting those men to protect them from sexual violence from non-white men. The promise is not safety but the preservation of their white privilege. Feminist philosopher Susan Griffin refers to this type of thinking as the patriarchal 'protection racket',[46] wherein men protect women from other men (protection which of course comes with strings attached). In far-right communities, particularly among far-right women, the trappings of benevolent sexism are often conflated with women's empowerment and value, while shedding the context of women's repression which necessitated it. For example, women now being expected to pay their way in relationships, as opposed to men financing the courtship, is spun as feminism having conned women out of being materially romanced, while ignoring the context of women's economic repression (including, in many contexts, not being able to have our own income or bank accounts).

As well as being anti-immigrant and Islamophobic, the misogyny of the aforementioned rhetoric is twofold. First, it objectifies women as things that need to be saved, or prizes to be won, in the struggle against the threat to the white race. Second, it often feeds into the far-right narrative that all women are promiscuous and sexually undiscerning, throwing themselves at the nearest alpha-male. Austrian psychoanalyst Wilhelm Reich theorised that fascism is psychosexual, an extension of cis men's sexual anxieties.[47] Controlling (cis) women's sexual and bodily autonomy is a core tenet of all far-right movements, from curtailing access to birth control and abortion for white women to the state-sanctioned sterilisation of women of colour and disabled women. In the far right's worldview, women's hypergamy (only dating or marrying above their own SMV) 'may be bad for men – their sexual needs are unfairly not met – but for the white race as a whole it is catastrophic. [...] like this, sexual anxiety becomes racial politics', note Moore and Roberts in *Post-Internet Far Right*.[48]

Fascist feminism

As with the men in these movements, women in the alt-right and far right are not homogeneous. While the majority of the most visible far-right women do believe in, or at the very least shill, either women's submission to men or women's role as wives, mothers, home-makers and caregivers as either being subordinate to or complementing men's position as patriarchs, leaders and warriors (an ideology known as 'complementarianism'), not all agree. While infiltrating far-right Telegram groups, some of the most interesting I found were small channels run by women (or people posing as women) who were open and self-identified racists but who were disgusted with the misogyny of their male peers. One channel, called WhiteFem (166 subscribers as of December 2022, before the group went private and banned Ava in the process), appears to be run by Sinéad McCarthy, the wife of Kyle Hunt. Together, the pair ran *Renegade Broadcasting*, a far-right podcast and radio show, as well as other far-right media productions. As of writing, they own the supplements company Heathen Herbals. In her channel, McCarthy laments the behaviour of white supremacist men. A meme shared in the channel shows a collection of white female wojaks – a type of crudely drawn person common in memes – being confronted by caricatures of shocked white men, their mouths agape, asking, 'Who radicalised you?' 'You did', reply the stoic white women, in a parody of a similar far-right meme, in which the same conversation plays out between stoic white men and caricatures of 'normies'.

In another message in the same group, McCarthy thanks the 'r******d' [uncensored in original] white nationalist movement for 'pushing [her] into feminism'. 'I never had any interest in feminism until I received so much abuse and harassment from men in these circles', she writes. McCarthy regularly cross-posts from a similar group, White Feminism (534 subscribers in January 2022, however the group no longer appears to be available). 'I was never interested in feminism and feminist theory until I got involved in pro-white politics and saw how even good men will tolerate violent levels of woman hatred when women don't raise hell about it', posted the anonymous owner of the group. I found five or so groups dedicated to posting about 'racist feminism' or the militaristic strength of white women. The groups were generally a fraction of the size of other far-right and white supremacist Telegram groups, with subscribers ranging from around 100 to 500, compared to other more orthodox channels which usually have thousands of subscribers.

So the role of women in the alt-right and far right is something of a paradox. Women are expected to only be wives and mothers yet the movement needs visible women to add a veneer of respectability. Women are sexualised and objectified and slut-shamed, yet they

are resented for their attractiveness and lack of avail-
ability to men. Just because the movement tolerates
some women in positions of authority, this doesn't
mean they actually have any power. Emily Gorcenski,
a data researcher and activist who created the site
First Vigil, which tracks trial information about white
nationalists, explains to me in an interview:

> We have to understand that identity-based forms of
> oppression are not purely rooted in discrimination.
> They are rooted in subordination. It's possible for, for
> example, a Jewish person or a Black person to join what
> is otherwise considered a white power movement.
> Because if they're willing to act in the service of white
> supremacy, those white supremacist groups are often
> more than willing to accept them [to further their own
> ends]. Even just allowing them into that circle is an act
> of dominance over that person.

Women's place in the alt-right and contemporary
far right is no different, she tells me. The women in
these movements, no matter how visible, exist only
as objects, shields to guard against accusations that
the movement is anti-woman, objects of sexualisation
or incubators with which to continue that white race.
However, we must be careful not to deny the autonomy of these women. Although they are victims of
misogyny (and often violence) within these communities, women in the far right must still be held accountable for the harm they do through furthering bigoted
beliefs, fighting for state intervention that will limit
the freedoms and dignity of marginalised people, and
inciting stochastic and scripted violence. Chip Berlet,

an investigative journalist and research analyst whose work focuses on right-wing extremism and conspiracy theories, describes this as the process 'by which a leader need not directly exhort violence to create a constituency that hears a call to take action against the named enemy'.[49] We must also remain aware that while they are often erased from wider conversations, marginalised women will bear the brunt of the far right's rise to power.

4

Feminism is cancer: how women are radicalised online

I thought I had it together mentally. I thought I was normal. I had a job, I was a normal person. But you don't know until you're in it.

Lucy Brown is telling me about how she became a videographer for Rebel Media, a Canadian far-right alternative news outlet, travelling the country to produce – in her own words – 'fake news' for Tommy Robinson. Before her journey into the far right, Brown had considered herself a leftist. She had even attended a meeting of the feminist group Sisters Uncut, though she came away from it feeling she had been 'silenced' and 'ostracised for being white'. Her first interaction with alt-right content was watching videos from Trump rallies, which she says 'spiralled' into watching other types of video.

She was particularly interested by the group Black Voices for Trump, who kept showing up in the background of the rally videos she consumed. 'They were talking about the treatment they've gotten. And I was like, hang on a second. These movements I've been in are condoning racism that I can't even fathom.'

The movements she's referring to here are Black Lives Matter (BLM) and other social justice groups, whom she considered racist because of their refusal to acknowledge the views of Black conservatives. This is a common argument made by the far/wider right – that refusing to let them say bigoted or intolerant things is the real bigotry or suppression of speech. Thus, Black, queer, feminist, etc. groups protesting or campaigning against hate speech are presented as anti-white, anti-family or anti-men.

From there, she began listening to alt-right podcasts and watching videos of people such as Milo Yiannopoulos during the day while at her job as a video editor. 'I was in the office late on my own, just watching it. Then it's like a drug, isn't it? You're like, oh, I'll watch another one.'

Brown's story is not uncommon. At least, the story she tells about herself is not uncommon. As we cover in this chapter, many women like her have gone down internet conspiracy rabbit holes as an answer to the frustration, boredom and discontentment in their lives. What greets them is a spiralling web of tunnels, consisting of algorithmic suggestions and human nudges. You've likely fallen down an internet rabbit hole yourself. Perhaps it was theories about a celebrity's relationship status that took you from Instagram to Reddit to Google to YouTube, pouring over posts and news coverage for answers. Perhaps it was playing 'wiki-linking', scrolling through Wikipedia clicking random links and reading entries to pass the time.

Maybe it was getting lost in the forum for a hobby or community that you'd never heard of, fascinated by their slang and in-jokes.

'Rabbit holes are ultimately just a series of links clicked in succession, and built into the design of social media', explain the authors of *Meme Wars: The Untold Story of the Online Battles Upending Democracy in America*. 'This design confers incredible power on people able to harness what we call the four Rs of media manipulation: repetition, redundancy, responsiveness, and reinforcement.'[1] Internet rabbit holes are not necessarily a bad thing but they can be a tool for radicalisation. This chapter explores how women are funnelled towards extremist far-right content, as well as the role women themselves play in creating these funnels. We also dig into some of the academic theory and debate around 'digital radicalisation' and whether this looks different for men and women.

Conceptualising radicalisation

Radicalisation is a long process that can't be completed through the internet alone. It's often conceptualised as a spectrum that is wider and more populous at the less extreme end and gets narrower and less populous, but more violent, the further along you go. (The literature on radicalisation uses a range of metaphors to describe this process, including pyramids, stairs, icebergs and funnels. I'll mostly be sticking to the pipeline metaphor for ease, except for when I'm quoting other sources or where it would be more appropriate to use a different metaphor.)

At one end are the people who commit terrorism or acts of violence such as mass shootings. The Barcelona Centre for International Affairs notes that only a small minority of radicals use violence to attract media attention, while the majority are not visible and use non-violent methods, which are more effective at achieving their goals. Among these less visible extremists 'there is a support base which occasionally agrees with the actions of the most committed militants and an even larger "silent minority" with a distaste for targeting non-combatants'.[2]

It's important to note that the vast majority of right-wing terrorists are men, with Anders Behring Breivik, Dylann Roof and Robert Gregory Bowers being some of the most notorious of the past few decades. Nonetheless, although women are less likely to ascend to the final tier of radicalisation, female terrorism is not completely unheard of.

Therefore, when we talk about radicalised women or women in the far right, we're mostly talking about people who are in the less visible majority of extremists. They use methods that are not directly violent to further hateful beliefs or to encourage or facilitate violence in others. They propagandise, act as tacticians and help radicalise others. Women's roles within the far right have mainly been as figures of propaganda, adding a veneer of respectability that helps normalise and spread their hateful ideologies. Women also do a lot of the reproductive labour in the far right, as within wider society: they organise rallies and community events, letter-writing campaigns and other acts of non-violent disruption (although the rallies they organise and attend can certainly turn violent, as with Charlottesville and 6 January). Like in mainstream society, these contributions often go unnoticed and uncredited, by both the men in these communities and the men who report on them. There are also far-right women who are even less visible, those who hold far-right views but do not act on them in any way. Others may partake in far-right communities, from regularly visiting websites or joining hate-filled Telegram groups to attending Evangelical churches, without necessarily contributing to violence or furthering the movement. Because of this, it's difficult to know the real extent of women in the far right, or even the size of the far right in general.

While most researchers agree that the internet has made the top of the radicalisation funnel much wider, helping groups recruit people they may not have otherwise had access to, most also agree that someone cannot go through the entire radicalisation process via the internet alone. In-person connections with recruiters are still needed in order to incite acts of terrorism. 'The internet may act as an "echo chamber" for extremist beliefs; in other words, the internet may provide a greater opportunity than offline interactions to confirm existing beliefs', write the authors of 'Radicalisation in the Digital Era', a 2013 report by RAND Europe. They go on to say, 'the internet is not a substitute for in-person meetings but, rather, complements in-person communication'.[3] This suggests that while the internet is an extremely powerful tool for recruitment and radicalisation, in-person contact is still necessary for a person to reach the level of terrorist.

However, thanks to the proliferation of the concept of 'leaderless resistance' on the right, there has been a significant increase in 'lone wolf' shooters, predominantly in America, in the last two decades. The term 'leaderless resistance' was popularised by white supremacist activist Louis Beam Jr in an essay of the same name. In it, Beam argues that organised groups are at risk of state infiltration and disruptions. He calls for 'non-organisation' instead: autonomous individuals or small cells (known as 'phantom cells') that operate autonomously and without central leadership.[4]

The methods used by the far right to groom young, frustrated, mostly white men via online forums and murky, semi-private dark socials is pretty well documented. Many come through anti-feminist routes, as we saw in previous chapters. 'Reading through the posting history of individual aliases, it's possible to chart their progress from vague dissatisfaction, and desire for social status and sexual success, to full-blown adherence to a cohesive ideology of white supremacy and misogyny', notes journalist Abi Wilkinson in a write-up about the manosphere. 'Neofascists treat these websites as recruitment grounds. They find angry, frustrated young men and groom them in their own image.'[5]

Anti-feminism is a powerful tool in the far right's armoury, given that 'it is calculated to appeal to the demographic overwhelmingly responsible for mass shootings: young white men'.[6] Places where misogynists gather act as incubators for terrorists, and violence against women is the number one predictor of mass shooters. But anti-feminism and the manosphere are not the only routes into the alt-right and far right for men. Others include white supremacy, anti-immigration and antisemitic rhetoric. Research has shown that the far right deliberately targets digital spaces such as gaming and bodybuilding forums, lobbies, subreddits and discords (Discord is an instant messaging platform where people can communicate via text or calls) as recruiting grounds. 'With recruitment now moving from physical gyms to chat rooms, livestreamed fights, tournaments, festivals, and even combat sports video games, we're seeing extremist fighting culture being combined with an entertainment culture that already valorizes violence and hypermasculinity',[7] writes Cynthia Miller-Idriss, who runs PERIL. Much has been written about men's radicalisation and its effect on modern politics, so we'll leave this outside the scope of this book.

Women's radicalisation

Women make up some of the most prominent alt-right and far-right influencers, yet their journey into the movement has, historically, been much less clear.

This is because of the ambivalent and benevolent sexism that erases women from political narratives, devalues the roles of women in social movements and presumes that women are more prone to acceptance and progressiveness, and in turn less prone to bigotry and violence. It is also because of the ways in which white supremacy benefits white women, painting them as kind, docile and innocent, whereas women of colour are more likely to be seen as aggressive and deviant. The attention paid to so-called ISIS brides compared to the white women who abandon their lives for white nationalist men is one example. This chapter explores the history of some of the most salient FFIs and propagandists, as well as the digital mechanism that aided in the radicalisation of women, in order to better understand what the process looks like.

Lauren Southern: alt-right poster girl

Lauren Southern is perhaps the most well-known female face of the far right. She started making right-wing YouTube videos when she was just 19. Her first video, called 'Lauren Southern: Why I'm Not a feminist', propelled her to fame – as of writing it is still live on the Rebel News YouTube channel and has 1.2 million views. In a follow-up video, Southern filmed herself at a feminist rally holding a sign saying 'There is no rape culture in the West' and confronting women attending the march, including survivors of sexual violence. 'Many prominent far-right men [who saw the video] said "wow, we have this new, firebrand woman and she's young and she's charismatic. Why don't we use her?" And she got elevated [from there]', explains journalist Daniel Lombroso, who spent several years shadowing the YouTuber for his documentary *White Noise*.

After being noticed, Southern was offered a job at Rebel News, where her skills as a blogger meant her career and profile ballooned. 'It's a similar pattern with Faith Goldy, who is another far-right woman who worked at Rebel News', adds Lombroso. 'Many of these other women get elevated much more quickly than the men because there were so few of them and having them be [visible is] so important to the narrative.' Rebel Media and other alternative media outlets such as Breitbart and Infowars act as incubators for media personalities and influencers within the 'alternative influence network' (AIN). The researcher Rebecca Lewis, who coined the term, describes the AIN as: 'an assortment of scholars, media pundits, and internet celebrities who use YouTube to promote a range of political positions, from mainstream versions of libertarianism and conservatism, all the way to overt white nationalism'.[8]

Sites such as Rebel News provide alternatives to mainstream media (often referred to as MSM), which many influencers distance themselves from in order 'to appeal to young, disillusioned media consumers', according to Lewis. They do this by dismissing traditional media's credentials, such as objectivity, neutrality and being the gatekeeper of legitimacy. 'Instead, they build trust with their audiences by stressing their relatability, their authenticity, and their accountability to those audiences.'[9] Lewis notes that they also provide a sense of social identity for those 'who feel like social underdogs for their rejection of progressive values'. For example, a pop-up on Rebel News warns users not to get censored, instructing them that 'Big Tech is censoring us. Sign up so we can always stay in touch.' Presenting themselves as alternatives to mainstream media, these sites in part legitimise influencers by providing a platform for their views and content.

Before being catapulted to far-right fame, Southern grew up in a diverse and metropolitan city in Canada (Surrey, in British Columbia). When she was in middle school, her father became frustrated at what he perceived as being an outsider in his community because of his whiteness and moved the Southern family to one of the whitest cities in Canada. Often in the radicalisation process, there is what's referred to as a 'catalyst event', something that shocks or destabilises the person enough for them to question their worldview or seek out answers to grievances – whether legitimate or not – they have with the world. 'This shocking event or personal crisis shakes an individual's certitude in previously held beliefs, prompts them to re-assess their entire life and become open to a radical change of values and behaviour',[10] writes Diego Muro, who researches terrorism at the University of St Andrews. For Southern, this was a teacher allegedly dividing her class by race and telling the children of colour, 'You're oppressed', and the white children, 'You're privileged' (the teacher has denied that this event took place). You've probably heard of 'catalyst events' under another, more colloquial name started by the alt-right, which is now ubiquitous on the internet: getting 'red-pilled'. Each female far-right influencer has their own red pill story (although the reality, as we explore through this chapter, is not always so straightforward).

Lana Lokteff: the darling of conspirituality

White nationalist YouTuber Lana Lokteff claims her red pill moment was hearing the Muslim call to prayer in Bethlehem and what she perceived as 'anti-white sentiment' within the media. But in *Sisters in Hate*, Seyward Darby suggests that Lokteff's radicalisation might not have been as sudden as she makes out. Lokteff spent much of her teens and early twenties listening to conspiracy-peddling radio stations with her brother. At first, these radio stations flirted with the bizarre and seemingly benign alternative belief systems of 1990s grunge and stoner culture: flat Earthers, lizard people and anti-vaccine guests were among the mainstay. But slowly, the sinister core of these beliefs unfurled over the airwaves. The 'lizard people' always seemed to be Jewish, the truth about Earth's flatness was obscured by a group of global elites – another dog whistle for Jewish people – and anti-vaccine conspiracies nearly always gave way to other anti-science stances that pointed the finger of blame firmly, once again, at a secret society of Jewish 'elites'.

Even in the early days of Lokteff's interest, as she dabbled in grunge in her teens, the radio show *Coast to Coast* hosted William Pierce, author of *The Turner Diaries* – a speculative fiction about a white supremacist insurrection in the United States that has been described as 'the bible of the racist right' by the FBI – who was allowed to share his views unchallenged. Whether Lokteff listened to this particular broadcast is unclear, but it does demonstrate the groundwork laid by these fringe media outlets. Eventually, Lokteff began conversing with the host of one of these shows, Henrik Palmgren, founder of the far-right multimedia company Red Ice. They hit it off and Lokteff moved to Sweden to be with him. They got married, Lokteff fully converted to paganism, and she became the brains – and voice – behind one of the most prolific white supremacist media outlets in the world, *Radio 3Fourteen*.

'Established in 2012, Radio 3Fourteen is a talk radio program hosted by Lana, heavily focusing on European identity and culture', reads the Red Ice website (interestingly, 2012 is the year Lokteff cites as the beginning of her 'rightward shift'). Lokteff's journey transported her from the peripheries of the 'keep Portland weird' grunge scene of the 1990s to the heart of the post-internet far right as one of the most prolific voices of white nationalism.

Candace Owens: 'leaving the left'

Another notable female influencer is Candace Owens, who claims her red pill moment was getting doxxed during Gamergate, when she ran her own doxxing site, SocialAutopsy.com. 'We're just trying to make people remember that they're human',[11] Owens told the *CTPost* in 2016, in an interview which now feels jarring to read. In it, she explains that she launched the website as a way to 'make the Internet a kinder place', following an incident of racial bullying she was subjected to during high school. A year after launching the site, she created a YouTube channel to share her right-wing views.

Although it is still unknown who doxxed her, Owens blamed liberals, which earned her support from right-wing commentators Milo Yiannopoulos and Mike Cernovich. 'I became a conservative overnight [...] I realized that liberals were actually the racists. Liberals were actually the trolls [...] Social Autopsy is why I'm conservative',[12] she said in 2017. By this time, she was working as communication director of Turning Point USA, an astroturfed student campaign (an orchestrated campaign designed to seem like a grassroots organisation) that aimed to 'identify, educate, train, and organize students to promote the principles of freedom, free markets, and limited government' – in layman's terms, it existed to promote conservative and Republican interest on American campuses. To this end, it runs a professor and school board watch list. In 2019, Owens also launched her Blexit campaign, which aimed to discourage Black Americans from voting Democrat (Owens credits Nigel Farage's Brexit campaign as her inspiration[13] – the former UK Independence Party leader was even invited to her wedding to George Farmer, son of a Tory peer, chairman of Turning Point UK and CEO of alt-tech platform Parler).[14]

Stories of 'leaving the left' such as Owens's are powerful currency among the far right, particularly when they come from women and minorities. Often, these stories involve discrediting feminist, civil rights and social justice movements by claiming that they are really responsible for holding back marginalised communities, while the right/far right offers real empowerment and freedom to oppressed people. (On its website, for example, Breitbart claims to have 'a strong track record of promoting women and minorities' and a more diverse masthead than many mainstream media titles.) Many of the most influential far-right female figureheads have leveraged their 'leaving the left' stories, including Owens and Ayla Stewart (Wife with a Purpose). Stewart claims to have once been a queer, polyamorous, new-age spiritualist, but after a traumatic childbirth she converted to Mormonism (before eventually leaving the Mormon Church) and dedicated her life to 'biblical womanhood'. Stewart became one of the most prominent female voices in the far right in the run-up to Trump's election in 2016. 'I was a former college liberal back in my college days, 15 years ago, and through having a large, Christian family I had seen the errors of liberal ideology first hand', writes Stewart in a closure notice on her blog. 'That made me danger-ous.' She further utilised her story as a reformed liberal by describing herself as a 'former SJW' (social justice warrior) in her (now banned) Twitter bio.

There is even an Instagram account, Fearless Femi-ninity, run by Bernadine Bluntly, which is in part dedi-cated to collating these types of stories. On her page, Bluntly shares stories from women claiming to have once been liberals, progressives or leftists 'reclaiming' their 'power' as feminine women. Often these accounts begin with the person rattling off a list of 'progressive' identities, with many saying they previously identified as queer (including claiming to be detransitioned trans-mascs/men), sexually promiscuous feminists. Many include allusions to struggling with mental illness. Next, the women share who they are now, which often includes listing characteristics and identities such as 'Christian' and 'feminine'. They always indicate they have been 'saved' or 'freed' from feminism and are – of course – much happier now.

'I grew up in a Christian family so I understood the Bible with my mind since I was a young child because of my parent's faith. But I was not walking with God until I was 19. Before that I was very depressed, sui-cidxl, and a feminist', reads part of one such story from a girl called Alina, posted on 17 March 2023. 'Suicidxl' is algospeak (coded language used to avoid moderation algorithms), partly obscuring the word in order to avoid being flagged by Instagram. In another post, a young girl called Olive claims she identified as demisexual before the pandemic and 'dressed and acted masculine'. 'I didn't like children obviously and I never planned on having any. I hated the idea of "submitting" to my husband. I wanted to be the dominant one', says Olive, who claims that her family became increasingly Conservative during the pandemic. While she was 'mad' at first, she 'started doing her own research and realised how brain-washed [she] was'. 'I noticed how unhappy other feminists were and how unhappy I was.' This plays into the narrative that feminism is the real oppressor of women and that traditional gender roles liberate women by allowing them to return to their 'true nature'. Bluntly, who runs the account (as well as another Instagram, TikTok and Telegram channel), also has an author's page on Evie, a Peter Thiel-funded media venture that aims to '[affirm] your femininity, encourages virtue, and offers a more truthful perspective than the biased agenda of other publications', according to their website – although it doesn't appear she's actually written anything for them.

Down the rabbit hole

When someone has their red pill moment and starts seeking out content online to re-enforce their worldview, they are met by a diverse and deliberate content funnel, facilitated by the far right. Emily Gorcenski explained to me over Zoom that 'there's a very strong content pipeline, and there's a very active but loosely connected network of people generating this type of content and they're targeting it all over the place. They're targeting women. They're targeting teen girls. They're targeting it to children of every gender [and] they're targeting it to older folks.' These 'pipe-lines', as they've come to be known, are not as simple as being directed from one site to another (although, in some cases, they might be). They are more like a system of algorithmic and intentional human nudges, guiding someone to more and more extreme content. As Joe Whittaker, Programme Director of Cyber Threats at Swansea University, argues, recommendation systems may help to create ideological filter bubbles, but users' own choices, including how they interact with recom-mended content, plays as much of a role.[15]

Probably the most written about example is that of YouTube, and the way in which its 'Leanback' feature – which autoplays another, similar video after one has ended – serves up increasingly extreme versions of whatever type of video someone started with. Because of this, Zeynep Tufekci, Professor of Sociology and Public Affairs at Princeton University, called YouTube 'one of the most powerful radicalizing instruments of the 21st century'.[16] In 2019 the *New York Times* reported that YouTube's autoplay feature was suggest-ing videos of partially clothed children after videos of sexual content (of performers of legal age) to paedo-philes.[17] Jessie Daniels, author of *Nice White Ladies*, captures the mechanism by which algorithms such as YouTube's disseminate hate speech:

Algorithms deliver search results for those who seek confirmation for racist notions and connect newcomers to like-minded racists, as when Dylann Roof searched for 'black on white crime' and Google provided racist websites and a community of others to confirm and grow his hatred. Algorithms speed up the spread of White supremacist ideology, as when memes like 'Pepe the Frog' travel from 4chan or Reddit to mainstream news sites. And algorithms, aided by cable news networks, amplify and systematically move White supremacist talking points into the mainstream of political discourse.[18]

In his widely read essay 'Something Is Wrong on the Internet', James Bridle explores a spiralling world of algorithmically led – and even generated – videos aimed at children which become increasingly disturbing and violent, including examples where beloved British cartoon character Peppa Pig drinks bleach and cannibalises her father. He likens these videos to merch created by bots from search engine optimisation (SEO)-driven 'unchecked list of verbs and pronouns with an online image generator' which contain slogans such as 'Keep Calm and Rape a Lot'.[19] These bots create content which is numerically boosted by other bots and served up to the perfect, undiscerning consumer: children. With their sticky thumbs on their mummy's iPad, children mash in search terms like 'Peppa Pig' or 'Egg Surprise', and, unbeknownst to them and their busy parents, are sent down a rabbit hole of self-radicalising bots and human actors with the goal of generating ad revenue (for whom is unclear).

'Automated reward systems like YouTube algorithms necessitate exploitation in the same way that
capitalism necessitates exploitation', writes Bridle.[20]
Similar mechanisms are at play when teens search
terms such as 'anti-feminism' or 'how to keep a boyfriend' on their iPhones. Up until now, the content
served up in answer to these searches has at least been
created by humans (although how SEO driven it is has
been surprisingly underexplored), but that may not
always be the case. While doing this research, I stumbled across a screenshot of a deeply transmisogynistic
poem written by ChatGPT and posted in a British white
nationalist Telegram channel. Convinced it was fake,
I shared it with my friend Eddie Ungless, a researcher
studying how human bias is recreated in machine
learning. He was eventually able to get ChatGPT to
create similar poems, suggesting that the screenshot
was real. As artificial intelligence (AI) software such
as ChatGPT, Bard and Dall-E become more accessible,
auto-generated memes, videos, blogs and other content
promoting extremist views may proliferate to the point
where, as with the cannibal Peppa Pig, they end up in
a self-radicalising feedback loop – the content of which
is created and perhaps even consumed by no one.

As with other forms of technology, including the
radio and internet, the far right have been early adopters of AI. A report by the Middle East Media Research
Institute (MEMRI) found that 'for neo-Nazis and white
supremacists in particular, [AI] is a key weapon in their
online arsenal, and they have very effectively deployed

AI-generated content as a disruptor in both mainstream online spaces and on their own channels'.[21] The report goes on to note that right-wing extremists are using AI to translate speeches from Nazis or to produce short, shareable summaries of far-right terrorist manifestos. However, it is AI's burgeoning video capabilities that MEMRI describes as the 'greatest security threat', particularly the ability to generate 'deep fake' videos of celebrities and political figures in order to erode trust and spread misinformation.

Speaking to *Wired* about the MEMRI report and the far right's increased usage of AI in its propaganda, Adam Hadley, the Executive Director of Tech Against Terrorism, said that the technology is being used in two ways: first, to create and manage bots that operate fake accounts; and second, to generate images, text and video at a far larger scale than was previously possible. A popular meme which has been circulating throughout British far-right and nationalist spaces shows a young white soldier in a First World War uniform on a bus. He peers into the 'camera' in a way reminiscent of the widely circulated photo of a US Marine referred to as having a 'thousand-yard-stare' due to his glazed and dissociated look. Behind him, a mass of Black and Brown men scream and seethe. One holds aloft a newspaper with the headline 'BRITISH TO TOE [*sic*] BE MINORITY'. When Britain First shared the meme in their Telegram channel they captioned it: 'Our war heroes have been betrayed. They would turn in their graves if they could see this country now.'

At least while there are humans still at the wheel, these networks generate different types of content and spread across the internet to create interconnecting pipelines. In her report on AIN, Rebecca Lewis explains that far-right influencer and media networks use strategies similar to content and influencer marketing, including using SEO techniques to capture eyeballs. She writes that 'content creators of the Alternative Influence Network use the techniques of online influencer culture not only to gain trust with their audiences but also explicitly to promote reactionary ideology. This reflects the larger phenomenon of online influencer marketing: microcelebrities on social media develop highly intimate relationships with their followers before inserting advertisements and marketing items into their content.'[22] But instead of inserting adverts for meal kits or therapy apps, these influencers are using the trust they've gained with their audience to hawk far-right ideas. 'Usually the influencer provides for the swarm a degree of articulation of their politics', write Moore and Roberts in their book *Post-Internet Far Right*, referring to an influencer's nebulous mass of followers as 'the swarm'. 'They make explicit what their members believe but are unable to say themselves.'[23]

These human nudges are more sporadic and less crushingly disinterested than the opaque algorithms of YouTube, TikTok and Pinterest. Instead, they take the form of helpful commenters on subforums answering your questions with links to news stories that will 'open your eyes', memes about immigrants being put up in five-star hotels which pop up in your feeds between pictures of Molly-Mae Hague and your cousin's new baby, people inviting you to Discord servers or livestreams discussing how hormonal birth control makes you less feminine.

One example of these human nudges comes to us from Mumsnet. Once considered a go-to forum for parenting advice, Mumsnet has become a hive of transphobia and a meeting point for the British gender critical movement, earning it the nickname 'Prosecco Stormfront'. In a post in the 'Woman's Rights' subforum (where the majority of transphobia takes place – other subforums such as 'Baby Names' and 'Parenting' seem to generally still be about issues related to raising children) entitled 'Do you ever wonder, what else have I been horribly wrong on all this time?' user JaneorEleven shares how her gender critical views have made her question her previous leftist beliefs.

'All my life I've been solidly left-leaning, and pretty much agreed with most points on the left', she writes, before concluding, 'Now I don't think I'm a closet right winger, but is it possible I've allowed the left to lead me up the garden path on other issues too?' The post, which has 278 replies as of writing, is full of commenters sharing how their transphobic views led them to question other 'progressive' or 'leftist' (as they describe them) positions, notably on the BLM campaign, Rotherham (referring to the alleged Muslim grooming gangs in Rotherham, a favourite talking point for

Tommy Robinson and Britain First) and Brexit. Littered throughout the comments are people sharing links to other sources that helped them 'see the light', such as an article on the far-right news outlet *Spiked* entitled 'Black Lives Matter's Missing Billions' (the article itself sources its claims from the *Daily Signal*, an offshoot of The Heritage Foundation).

'Once you perceive something, you can't go back, and then you ask more questions, and it unravels a bit more', another user replies with regard to the *Spiked* link. This discussion thread not only illuminates the way in which transphobia facilitates conspiratorial thinking and radicalisation but also one of the tactics employed by the far-right: 'educating' people who are 'just asking questions' by providing biased sources. 'Just asking questions', sometimes colloquially called JAQing off, is a tactic used by right-wing trolls to destabilise an argument with leading questions, laying the burden of proof on the other person. It is a favourite of 'Groypers', a loose collection of white nationalists which grew out of podcaster Nick Fuentes's fan base.

'What we're seeing is that this is not a single, uniform strategy', Gorcenski tells me. Each far-right female influencer or network employs their own strategy or focal point. Many, such as Stewart and Huber, use themes such as traditional womanhood and blogging about homemaking. For others, such as Southern and Owens, the focus is more political. Others still, such as McCarthy and Kellie-Jay Keen-Minshull (aka Posie Parker) promote their ideology under the guise of 'women's rights'.

'With the US Capitol insurrection, there were quite a number of women who were either arrested or played central roles in the organising', says Gorcenski. 'That's [the result of] two very different types of radicalization. We also see lots of younger teenage and early twenties women engaging in some of this accelerationist content. The more violent is [neo-]Nazi content because it's the most edgy and it gets a lot of attention. So there are lots of different types of messaging.' Gorcenski adds that there's no single way in which women are drawn into these movements; the white supremacist movement has 'mastered the art of tailoring content' to appeal to people in different ways, without making it obvious that they're being sucked into a hate movement. 'Once you've hit that slippery slope, it's too late', she concludes. In Chapter 5, we explore some of the different types of content used to appeal to women in more depth.

The top of these pipelines often employs content that can be plausibly denied, either by claiming that it's ironic, or trolling, or in the case of a lot of content targeting women, 'just asking questions'. Several so-called debates, notably around the supposed threat that trans women or immigrant men pose to cis women's safety, have been used to manufacture culture wars within mainstream discourse. By framing the idea that minorities having equal rights and liberties is a threat to the majority – to their way of life, to their freedom of speech and even to common sense itself – the far right has legitimised its bigotry and created more pathways to lure people into extremist views.

From the mid-2010s, 'owning the libs' became the heart of political strategy for Republicans and conservatives. The historian Nicole Hemmer argues that 'owning the libs' acted as a substitute for the cohesive conservative ideology of the Cold War and held the American conservative voting block together in the absence of shared policy.[24] To further this, sociologist Scott Melzer posits that culture wars are created by conservative, reactive organisations and movements, where members possess a 'sense of victimisation at the hands of a liberal culture run amok'.[25]

As discussed in Chapter 3, Gamergate was seen as a test run for how well culture wars could work as a strategy for the far right, including by former Trump advisor and Breitbart co-founder Steve Bannon. Eviane Leidig has found that FFIs utilise culture wars in different ways to recruit and propagandise to men and women. The culture war around women's place and safety can be capitalised on both to direct scripted violence towards minorities and to create an 'in' group of traditional women. 'One particular strategy has been the showcasing of sisterhood within the far-right, with the hope of recruiting vulnerable, lonely young women who seek friendship', she explains to me over email. 'There have been discussions about recruiting women from different backgrounds, although the two main target groups are either "tradcaths" (i.e. women who grew up traditional and religious) or "recovering feminists" (i.e. women who were previously left-wing and now disillusioned).' The far right, then, claims to offer women a community where they don't have to compete with one another for men or jobs or protection (this, of course, never materialises, as far-right and white supremacist communities on and offline are deeply paranoid, fighting for limited attention from audiences and investors, and full of feuds).

Scrolling through the subreddit r/redpillwomen, you quickly find that many of the posts are from women seeking advice about their husbands or boyfriends, as opposed to discussing theory or politics. If you look past the use of terminology such as SMV, many of the posts wouldn't be out of place in a group chat: how to deal with jealousy, what gifts you need to get a husband, and – one of the most posted-about topics – how to find a boyfriend. 'It's the least toxic place for women on Reddit', says user Jenna_grows in response to the prompt: 'What made you joint [*sic*] this community/subscribe to this school of thought?' Despite saying that she is not 'fully RP' (red-pilled), she continues: 'The women here are genuinely helpful, practical, smart and honest. To me, this is what sisterhood is and I am inspired to be my best self, both in the real world and online.'

Another user, Magic_emoji, says she is a child-free woman working in tech and that the women in her workplace 'are really toxic feminists in a sense that they judge every woman who doesn't share their ideas about men and dating'. 'I rather don't go to this topic with them [*sic*] so I need a place where I can say things openly – and that's this sub! I honestly love how supportive and not judgemental women here are. It's sad to say but I feel more understood and accepted here than I feel at my females girlfriends [sic] circle.' Seeking community is one of the most prominent reasons why people will join extremist movements, often placing it above actual belief in the ideology. As the sociologist Kathleen Blee writes, 'social camaraderie, a desire for simple answers to complex political problems, or even the opportunity to take action against formidable social forces can coexist with, even substitute for, hatred as the reason for participation in organized racist activities'.[26]

One of the ways this type of content has been seeded across the internet is through relationship advice – specifically, advice that frames heterosexual relationships as binary and essentialist. While tradwives across social media might espouse anti-feminist or even seemingly anti-capitalist views, it's important to remember that sexual anxiety is still at the movement's heart, as it is with incels and those in the manosphere (although the two groups are not equivalent: the tradwife movement does not have body count). While the movement has evolved over the years, even in the time I've been writing this book, Julia Ebner traces its roots back to the subreddit r/redpillwomen, where women are taught that their only goal in life is to please men, meaning they must focus their energy on relationships and aspire to marriage.

Away from r/redpillwomen, relationship coaches on TikTok, Instagram, YouTube, Reddit and Twitter promise to teach women how to bag a 'high-quality' or 'alpha' man by stepping into their 'divine feminine energy' or embracing their 'dark femininity'.

'Send this video to your best friend or sister so we can all keep each other accountable and actually do these things', says TikTok user happyfitzam at the beginning of a video promising to teach women three ways they can embrace their divine feminine energy (the ways are: making something with your hands, being outside in nature and setting boundaries). Once again, we can see how influencers position themselves as community builders despite creating monodirectional content. This kind of divine feminine content has been accused of repackaging Christian gender ideals in new-age speak, as it often encourages women to allow men to 'step into their divine masculine' by becoming leaders and providers. This, the femininity coaches promise, will in turn allow you to step into your femininity, wherein you'll be softer, gentler, more permissible and, of course, happier. The trend also overlaps with the 'soft life' TikTok aesthetic, a short-lived trend where women shared videos encouraging each other to step away from the corporate grind in favour of a life more focused on the domestic sphere and leisure time. Many of the videos were almost identical to those created by tradwives. Divine feminine content also acts as a gateway for anti-hormone and new-age wellness content, which I explore in more depth in Chapter 5. In particular, though, women are encouraged to get back in touch with their natural cycle and allow their divine feminine energy to follow unimpeded by hormonal birth controls.

Pink-pilling

While these women claim to mostly be creating content for other women – as they often phrase it, 'creating a community' around traditional womanhood – they also attract a large male audience, sometimes larger than their female audience. Eviane Leidig points out that these female influencers play up to their male audience, creating vlogs and other types of content to attract men to their channels. They strive to become the archetype of wives, girlfriends and mothers for white nationalist and far-right men – to become something 'worth fighting for'.

In many of the Telegram channels run by far-right men, the tone is one of constant fear. Every day (sometimes up to 200 times a day) posts are shared about the coming white genocide, sexualised violence against children (often imagined at the hands of immigrants and queers) and tyrannical governments taking away your rights and culture. It's easy to see how these environments can lead to young men becoming nihilistic, giving up entirely on society and either turning to spree violence or suicide (often both simultaneously), a process which is referred to in the far right as becoming 'black pilled'.

'For Black Pill adherents seeking to change society rather than simply accept their fate, the use of mass violence to forcibly overthrow the system and force normies to take notice is positioned as a key pathway to structural change', explain Megan Kelly, Alex DiBranco and Julia R. DeCook for *New America*.[27] While black-pilling young men is the express goal of some online communities, it is not a useful tactic for organised far-right movements: kids that are locked up or dead can't vote or march or do banner drops. Plus, it isn't great for optics. These groups need to find a balance that creates a sense of urgency through fear without leading to complete despair.

This tactic is known colloquially as 'white-pilling', and while it's not just the job of women (or women's only role), women certainly are a useful tool. After all, with so many young men washing up in the far right via the manosphere or incel communities, the promise of women, or romance, or sex, or a blissful domestic sphere over which you get to be king, is a powerful incentive. Laura Towler, wife of Sam Melia and one of the directors of the UK far-right group Patriotic Alternative (PA), is a good example of this. There are multiple PA Telegram channels for different regions and purposes, and key figures in the group, including Laura, Sam and Mark Collett, have their own dedicated channels where they can post monodirectional updates.

For figures such as Mark and Sam, these generally consist of streams of videos and screenshots of news articles (mostly from the *Daily Mail*), fearmongering about violence allegedly carried out by immigrants, counter-protesters, queer (particularly trans and non-binary) people and people of colour, and COVID-19 conspiracies, occasionally interspersed with cross-posted updates about 'activism' carried out by local chapters. The aim is to create a sense of impending white replacement and chaos, wherein immigrants and people of colour run amok and white culture and the stability it supposedly offers is destroyed. Occasionally, Mark and Sam will post about their own lives, including videos of 'Great British Grub' or traditionally British activities.

At first glance, Laura's channel is similar. She posts or cross-posts the same scaremongering videos and articles, and occasionally she discusses her perspective as a white British wife and mother (that most venerated of statuses). Where her channel differs is the ratio of scaremongering to posting about her own life (she also posts far less regularly than either Mark or Sam, although still daily). As so much of her status rests on being a mother, Laura regularly talks about her husband Mark and their children, as well as their tea shop and products. Women must also provide levity and optimism in the face of the coming violence of the race war or white genocide. They are, after all, a prize rather than a comrade. They need to be the thing worth fighting for, every misogynist's wet dream: the mother you can fuck.

As part of courting men as an audience, Leidig says far-right movements turn to female far-right creators for inspiration on how to radicalise their wives, girlfriends and mothers.[28] In a video entitled 'How to Red Pill Women' (151,000 views, posted 10 May 2017), Rebecca Hargraves (aka Blonde in the Belly of the Beast) explains to the presumed male audience that the reason women are hesitant to reject 'feminism, globalisation and liberalism' and embrace 'traditional gender roles' is because 'we [women] have a disproportionate societal advantage'. This includes 'occupational advantages because of diversity initiatives', advantages in the family court system (a nod to a key talking point among certain factions of the manosphere) and people being 'generally afraid to restrict women in any way'.

Hargraves goes on to suggest that the male viewer could try pointing out to their partner that, 'despite having more power than they have ever had at any place or point in history', women are unhappier than ever. As we explored in the previous chapter, blaming feminism or liberalism for an increase in women's dissatisfaction, without acknowledging causes such as rising poverty, job insecurity and atomisation, is a favourite tactic among the far right. Hargraves proposes that the viewer introduce their partner to far-right YouTube personalities, crediting Black Pigeon Speaks for her own red pill moment. (In the video, which Hargraves has pinned, Black Pigeon Speaks comments: 'This is one of, if not THE most important tasks facing society today.')

Another example comes to us from Stormfront, which the SPLC describes as 'first major hate site on the Internet'.[29] Stormfront is a website and forum for neo-Nazis, where people can access racially charged alternative news, post opinions, connect with other users and even try to find a date. 'Whereas typical hate sites function as one-way transfers of information – rather like a brochure that can be read but not responded to – Stormfront has always been organised as a message board', notes the SPLC of the website's longevity and success.[30]

One long-running discussion thread, housed in the 'The Women's Forum', asks how white nationalism can appeal to more women. The thread originated in 2008, when a user with the handle Kaleen posted:

> I guess this is a two part question spawned from another thread that has since gone down memory lane for the female bashing that was going on there. So, now we can have our own discussion here, with no male influence. Please remember to keep it civil and no male bashing here. 1. What would attract more women to WN [white nationalism]? 2. What attracted you, personally, to WN?

The thread, which is pinned to the top of the forum for easy accessibility, has 482 replies and 289,574 views as of writing. 'Women are being taught it is "empowering" to reject femininity. [...] But modern society especially feminists attack women for having these views they are doing this because they have vile hatred towards men but are in denial about ALSO having vile hatred also towards women and children', reads one of the most recent replies. 'The Women's Forum', which has the tagline 'Sugar and spice, and everything nice', exists as a space for women to discuss issues relevant to them, including motherhood, shopping and home-making, but also their frustration at men and misogyny in the movement, all intermingled with violent racism and antisemitism.

'The women in the ladies only discussion saw themselves as both white supremacists and feminists and I took them at their word', writes Jessie Daniels in *Nice White Ladies*. 'Without an explicit challenge to racism, this kind of feminism becomes a usual device for furthering white supremacist goals. This is another way that white womanhood gets weaponised to protect "the ladies" and all that white womanhood supposedly represents.'[31]

From community building to stochastic terrorism

However, more and more FFIs are straying from the script of 'creating community' for other women and moving into a role of accelerationism and agenda-setting scripted violence. One of the most prominent and dangerous examples of this is Chaya Raichik, the woman behind Libs of TikTok. Raichik has created a far-right media empire which has been described as 'a wire service for the broader right-wing media ecosystem'.[32] The content shared across the Libs of TikTok channels, which include Telegram, Twitter, Instagram and a website, mostly focuses on reposting videos by LGBTQ+ content creators, especially teachers, with the intent of 'exposing' how 'gender ideology' is being pushed on children. Raichik has become one of the key voices in inciting scripted violence, which Moore and Roberts further describe in *Post-Internet Far Right* as violence which is 'modelled on the pronouncements of influencers or groups, which do not explicitly call for attacks but where violence is an implied solution or natural outcome'.[33]

Raichik is a key driver behind the increasing accusation that LGBTQ+ individuals, particularly trans people, are 'groomers'. This rhetoric has become so widespread that 'groomer' is now recognised as a slur against queer people. The Institute for Strategic Dialogue, a non-profit organisation dedicated to analysing and reporting on extremism, explains: 'In the US particularly, the use of this language, along with conspiratorial thinking around queer people, has led to legislation preventing the discussion of LGBTQ+ issues in schools and preventing trans children from accessing gender affirming healthcare, and has motivated attacks on LGBTQ+ individuals.'[34]

In September 2022, Raichik was implicated in claims of harassment against children's hospitals in Boston and Washington, DC. Threats against the two hospitals came after Raichik falsely accused both of performing hysterectomies on patients under 16. As a result, Boston Hospital was subjected to a hoax bomb threat. Writing for the SPLC, Cassie Miller calls threats against doctors providing (or even being accused of providing) gender-affirming care to kids 'an eerie echo of the kind used against medical professionals who provided abortions in the 1990s when activists declared that murdering abortion providers should be considered "justifiable homicide"'.[35]

How female far-right influencers take advantage of social media

The far right has always been ahead of the curve in terms of adopting new technology for spreading its rhetoric. Nazis uploaded entire manuscripts and databases of their propaganda to dial-up bulletin systems (DBS), precursors to the modern World Wide Web. As early as 1983, a white supremacist named George Dietz uploaded Holocaust denial literature to a DBS, spreading it to countries where it had previously been banned from being printed, such as Germany.[36] This trend of early adoption has continued throughout the rise of social media, from early forums to the current most popular network, TikTok.

The micro-video platform is one of the fastest-growing platforms, with 500 million active users per month (March 2023). Since its launch in 2017, TikTok has exploded in popularity and has already become a breeding ground for far-right content. One of its USPs is its 'For You Page', an infinite-scroll feed consisting of algorithmically powered suggestions from across the platform that the user may or may not choose to follow. There's also the 'Following' feed, where users can see content only from creators they've chosen to follow. But unlike YouTube, users do not choose which video to watch when; content is offered up in an endless stream. It's YouTube's 'lean back' algorithm on steroids.

'[O]n YouTube you can deactivate auto-play, ignore recommendations, and use the service just like Netflix to view specific videos you came to watch', writes Cameron Hickey for *Wired*. 'With TikTok the recommendation system is the interface. From the minute you enter the platform, you're riding through the wormhole. The serendipity of the next video is what makes TikTok special – but unchecked it may also serve to radicalise audiences more effectively than YouTube ever has.'[37] TikTok is also a visual medium, which as Leidig points out is a popular and effective tool for women in the far right. In the same article, Cameron explains why this method is so potent: 'What makes a TikTok video more potent than a hyperpartisan meme shared on Facebook or a retweeted #MAGA slogan? It's the intimacy. When you make a video on the platform, you're staring at a mirror image of yourself. You're having a personal conversation, just like FaceTiming a friend.'[38]

In 2024, the ISD released a study revealing the magnitude of white nationalist and neo-Nazi content on TikTok. They reported finding over 200 'pro-Nazi' accounts, with neo-Nazi content receiving tens of millions of views, in part thanks to algorithmic boosting. They also noted that TikTok was failing to take down such content, even when it had been flagged by users, and that videos from these pro-Nazi accounts often

featured AI-generated content. Perhaps most alarm-
ingly, they found evidence of videos sharing instruc-
tions on how to carry out real-world violence against
Jewish communities, posted on an account that sought
to move users to a 'secure group chat' for further
instruction.[39]

While most discussions around the radicalisation of
young people online focuses on platforms such as 8kun
and its predecessor 4chan, subreddits, Discord, Twitch
and gaming lobbies, female influencers seem to prefer
visual platforms such as YouTube and Instagram,
where they can doll up their hatred in a more feminine
aesthetic. Leidig notes that female far-right influencers are more likely to reach female audiences on platforms such as Instagram, one of the few social media
platforms with a female-dominated user base. In the
UK, women make up 57 per cent of the platform's user
base, compared to 42 per cent male users (numbers for
non-binary users were not available). Worldwide, the
difference was less pronounced: 'in the US, males lead
age groups 18–24 and 25–34'.[40]

Leidig points out that FFIs may build their audience
by first sharing content which 'isn't necessarily about
things like politics, but it's more about sort of documenting their everyday life'.[41] In doing so, FFIs position
themselves alongside typical influencers who use their
platform to review/promote products such as clothes
or make-up. As Rebecca Lewis notes, '[b]y emulating
techniques used by mainstream celebrities and fashion
bloggers on Instagram, they minimise the significance

of their racist views'.[42] She argues that AINs utilise influencer marketing strategies, 'but instead of selling products or services to their audiences, they sell political ideology'.[43]

The content produced by FFIs may also evolve over time, both towards and away from politics. 'Some of these influencers tend to discuss politics quite heavily', says Leidig. 'And then once they become mothers, which is the primary duty for women in the far right [...] a lot of their content will change to reflect that as well.' Here, again, we can see the forward-facing and backward-facing techniques used by Beal and Clark of Girl Defined, wherein far-right content creators tailor their content to both the specific platform they're using and the level of receptiveness to far-right or fundamentalist ideas the users of that platform may have.

The types of content FFIs produce to spread their ideology (or promote themselves, or make money) also varies across platforms. For example, Caitlin Huber (aka Mrs Midwest) is a tradwife content creator who tailors her messaging across different platforms. Huber talks more frankly about her political views on forums such as Reddit or her blog than she does on Instagram or YouTube, where she focuses on topics of femininity or motherhood (which lend themselves better to the visual platform than political theory does). While Huber's Instagram now mostly documents her life as a stay-at-home mother, her YouTube channel is dedicated to content 'teaching' women how to be more 'traditionally feminine', via videos entitled 'How to

Act Like a Lady to Achieve More Success!' (posted 9 October 2022) and 'How to Be "THAT" Feminine Girl ...' (posted 10 April 2022). Meanwhile, on her blog, she delves more into writing about 'biblical womanhood' and casually recommends far-right commentators such as Black Pigeon Speaks and Brittany Sellner (aka Brittany Pettibone), alongside travel vlogs and baking channels.

Joe Whittaker, Programme Director of Cyber Threats at Swansea University, argues that rather than conceptualising radicalisation as a binary between online and offline, it would perhaps be more meaningful to compare the ways people engage with extremist content across different types of platform.[44] Intuitively, we know that the dialect of different platforms can vary. For example, the kind of stream-of-consciousness style we use on X (formally Twitter) may not make it to our more curated Instagram grids. 'These platforms offer entirely different user experiences and have a different set of rules and realities', Whittaker writes. 'Rather than grouping all platforms as "online", it is more analytically useful to understand these user experiences in relation to each other as part of a wider environment. It is possible that there are more differences between some types of online communication than between online and face-to-face communication.'[45] I think that FFIs would make a strong sample group to study this, as they curate their persona of authenticity in a way that builds upon the rules and semantics of different platforms.

Visual mediums may give FFIs even more power to spread their message than their male counterparts. Studies have shown that conventionally attractive, thin, cis, white content creators are less likely to have their content struck down for breaching community guidelines and more likely to rise up the recommendation ladder.[46] This is because of the way human biases have seeped into the algorithms that silently dictate our social media experiences.

'The truth is that Instagram, like our society, is biased against anyone who doesn't look like Emily Ratajkowski or Nick Bateman', writes journalist Salma El-Wardany. 'If you step outside that mould, a subtle, coercive defensive is launched by Instagram's technology which involves shadow banning, flagged accounts and a breaching of community guidelines'.[47] Conventionally attractive white women such as Huber, Southern, Beal and Clark are less likely to have their content removed, no matter what kind of dog whistles they use in their captions, whereas people of colour, queer and disabled folks calling out discrimination or even just trying to post a selfie are more likely to have their posts moderated, creating an uneven playing field that reinforces the dominance of white, cis, straight, able-bodied people.

Influencers who are deemed likely to become mothers are rewarded by both the algorithm and brand sponsorship. 'Non-risky influencers – who are hired more frequently, and paid more – tend to be white, beautiful, heterosexual with long-term boyfriends who they will eventually engage, marry and procreate with', writes Sophie Bishop, an Associate Professor of Media Studies at the University of Keele. 'Then, of course, they become mommy bloggers. This is the expected life cycle of the influencer; the A-List beauty vloggers of the mid-2010s have gracefully aged out of beauty and fashion verticals, posting less and dropping followers.'[48] That's not to say FFIs are deemed 'non-risky'; influencers who shy away from politics, who don't take a stand or say anything that could be deemed controversial, are of course preferred by the majority of brands.

In order to understand the current state of the internet and influencer culture, one has to grasp the role that so-called mommy blogging has played in its development. Mommy bloggers were the precursor to affiliate links, which prop up so much of the contemporary internet's revenue generation (including for many major media outlets). This is because early motherhood bloggers would link out to products they used when discussing parenting.[49] In a way, FFIs mirror the ideal life cycle of an influencer. Their career is always arcing towards motherhood, no matter how political their content may be. The irony that motherhood as aspirational content is foundational to the contemporary internet landscape, one which helped shape the thought architecture of the alt-right and far right, and has now become a way in which the far right propagandises to women, is not lost on me. The internet has commodified motherhood, and now the far right sells it back to women as an escape from the capitalist grind. As Cynthia Miller-Idriss, a scholar of extremism and radicalisation, has noted, much of the tradwife movement is 'rooted in many young women's sense of discontent with mainstream society and capitalist systems that – in the US in any case – make balancing motherhood and work a near-impossible task, with virtually no childcare support, limited sick leave and few protections for women who need time away from work for childcare or eldercare responsibilities'.[50]

The far-right female influencer economy

Strip away the fairy-lit backdrops, cross-platform collaborations and double-speak and what you're left with is economics. A 2024 report by collabstr, a prominent influencer marketing platform, found that the influencer marketing industry is set to reach $19.8 billion by the end of 2024, up 13 per cent on 2023's revenue. It also found that female content creators dominate the industry, making up 70 per cent of the market share.[51] As with many other industries, the highest-paid spots still tend to go to men: only two of the ten most highly paid influencers in 2023 were women, according to Forbes.[52] However, visually led platforms – the kind favoured by FFIs – tended to be those that offered the highest earnings, with Instagram and TikTok being the most lucrative.

Mirroring the way in which economic instability is an often-cited factor in rising fascism and populism,

Emily Hund, author of *The Influencer Industry*, argues that the recession paved the way for the influencer boom. In an interview with *Vox*, she explains how the financial crash of 2007–2008, coupled with the increasing availability of the internet in people's homes, as well as the 'valorization of entrepreneurialism and self-branding' in the US, led to

> a very material financial break for many people and an ideological break for a lot of people as well, where they started to think, 'Wow, this system is not going to save me, and I have to do something to try to survive'. There was all this rhetoric about the wonders of social media, and it drove a lot of people online to try to keep themselves afloat in some way.[53]

Hund goes on to argue that sexism within workplaces, as well hostility towards parenthood, has made influencing and social media seem like a more appealing career for women. Building on this, women are more likely to be in precarious or gig employment, with one report from Lancaster University finding that women were nearly twice as likely as men to be in 'severely insecure employment' and noting that 'the situation worsens for mothers, disabled women, and women from Black, Pakistani and Bangladeshi backgrounds'.[54] The COVID-19 pandemic also had an asymmetric impact across gender, with women being more likely to be furloughed or made redundant. In 2020, female employment around the world declined by 4.2 per cent, according to the International Labour Organization.[55]

'Some of the hardest-hit sectors due to COVID-19 were those where the share of female employment relative to their total employment is higher than that for men', writes Akrur Barua, an Associate Vice President at Deloitte. 'In most economies, women are more likely to dominate sectors such as hospitality, food services, and personal care. ... [A]s people moved indoors to stay safe from the virus and many businesses turned to remote work, women generally took up a greater share of household chores than men.' He goes on to say that with less availability of childcare facilities that are vital to working mothers, as well as many schools turning to online lessons, keeping children in their homes, the majority of childcare duties fell on mothers.[56] The economic uncertainty of the pandemic may be driving women further right in their politics, back into domestic labour and deeper into the arms of the influencer economy.

From tradwives to tradcaths

Tradwife content in particular has exploded on TikTok (at the time of writing, the search term tradwife/tradwives has 47 million views on the platform), as have other forms of FFI-focused videos, including 'skull mask e-girls', in which young women don the e-girl look, which mixes the grunge and emo youth subcultures with gaming iconography and design (including neon lighting and cat-ear headsets) to create an irony-laced, internet poisoned aesthetic. 'E-girls and e-boys are what would happen if you shot a teenager through the internet and they came out the other side', explains *Vox*'s digital culture reporter, Rebecca Jennings.[57] E-girls (and boys) generally test the limits of 'edgy' internet humour, sharing cutesy memes alongside BDSM references. Given their participation in gaming culture, e-girl content is often met with accusations of interloping in male spaces for attention or being a 'fed' or propaganda.

Skull mask e-girls lean fully into this accusation, creating cutesy videos where they dance – or more often just stare into the camera at suggestive angles to music – wearing the skull mask, a snood emblazoned with a white skull jaw, a symbol associated with the neo-Nazi group Atomwaffen and the web forum Iron March. The several layers (or perhaps veneers) of irony at play in this subculture 'produces a genre of (mostly) TikTok accounts in which teenage girls perform the aesthetics of neo-Nazism, to an audience of boys and men who follow and interact with their content, often leaving derogatory comments', explains Hazel Woodrow of the Canadian Anti-Hate Network.[58] The bullying they receive from their audience may contribute to their radicalisation. 'They end up feeling a need, in a lot of circumstances, to up the ante and be more extreme in order to prove themselves and prove that they're not feds', Woodrow explains to me directly during an interview.

Bridging the gap (across all platforms) between the tradwives (a product of the pre-Trump and Trump years) and the skull mask e-girls (a distinctly Gen Z subculture existing at the very edge of plausible deniability) is the cultural milieu of tradcaths, or what fashion magazine *Coveteur*'s culture editor called 'hot girl Catholicism'.[59] While 'traditional Catholicism' refers to a specific subset of belief, which many adopters of the early online subculture were drawn to, the term has since broadened (as phrases the internet gets a hold of often do) to refer to anyone adopting the Catholic internet aesthetic regardless of beliefs. Straddling the downtown New York art scene (sometimes referred to as Dimes Square) and a digital network of podcasts and livestreams, the tradcath or 'femtroll' milieu is markedly more esoteric than its predecessor (tradwives or Evangelical womanhood). Write-ups in *Dazed*, *i-D* and *Vice* describe it using terms such as 'schizo-posting' and 'meta-irony'. Two key figureheads of the scene are *Red Scare* podcast hosts Dasha Nekrasova and Anna Khachiyan.

Red Scare was originally a pillar of the dirtbag left, a nominally socialist/leftist movement that organised around Democratic senator Bernie Sanders's presidential campaign in the run-up to the 2016 election. The dirtbag left differentiated itself from other leftist organising and thinking at the time by rejecting identity politics, which it saw as a distraction from workers' rights and financial issues. In practice, this often meant dirtbag leftists discarded or outright denigrated any issues relating to social, racial or gendered justice.

The *Red Scare* hosts rose to notoriety in part thanks to their liberal use of slurs, even in the early, self-proclaimed leftists days of the show. Now Nekrasova identifies as a traditional Catholic (i.e. one who rejects the liberalising reforms of the Second Vatican Council of 1962–1965) and uses her online presence to promote purity culture and regressive gender roles in a slurred, ironic tone. Khachiyan, meanwhile, tweeted 'Let's be clear on one thing: I am not and have never been a liberal or a leftist. I'm a cryptofascist, and the "crypto" is being generous' in 2015, although it's hard to know what level of 'irony' she thought she was operating on.

Although the exaggerated femininity of women such as Nekrasova means their religiosity is written off as shallow and inauthentic by some of the men in their movement, their conversion to, and espousing of, traditional Catholicism aligns them with an incredibly powerful force, one which is currently using its vast wealth and resources (including legal and lobbying) to attack rights to bodily autonomy such as gender-affirming healthcare and abortion in multiple countries, including the US and UK. Their views align with white supremacy in more theological ways too: 'Just as white supremacists reach back to a fictional version of the Middle Ages or the Viking Age to create their own mythos, the trads look back to an imagined pre-modern church', writes journalist Molly Olmstead.[60]

The rise of Catholicism in youth subcultures (although Nekrasova and Khachiyan are both in their thirties), including those that play on the edge of fascism, is reminiscent of the role paganism used to play more prominently in subcultures. It allows white people, but particularly white Americans, to feel connected to and identify with a culture, heritage and community beyond the white hegemony. In an exploration for *i-D* magazine, feminist writer Biz Sherbert argues that quasi-Catholic imagery has taken hold among America's alternative youth to fill the vacuum, now that wearing headdresses or bindis has been recognised as appropriative. 'Effectively, alt white kids have had to adapt and look for new ways to differentiate themselves from the sea of normies and basics. Trendsetters began to avoid ripping off styles from people of colour [...] and new reservoirs of the "unproblematic exotic" were scouted out and added to the alt lexicon', writes Sherbert. She continues, 'it's easy to see how a girl who got her star sign tattooed on her wrist in 2019 might pivot to trad-signalling in 2021 – underneath spiritually-saturated aesthetics is often a sideways yearning for a divine order that makes sense of a world that is casually cruel and unpredictable'.[61] Like paganism, Catholicism can easily be weaponised to promote the idea of 'white culture' and history as both superior and suppressed. If Lokteff discovered paganism and conspirituality through 1990s shockjock radio, young women today are converting to Catholicism and discovering anti-vax content through podcasts.

Online, many of these subcultures draw from the 'girlblogging' of the mid-2010s, using Tumblr-esque imagery of disaffected young women who are overwhelmingly white, shockingly thin and clad in childish clothing which is juxtaposed against hardcore sexual elements (think a 'daddy' T-shirt, pigtails and a ball gag). When I set up a Pinterest account for my sockpuppet Ava, I started by pinning a few pictures of siege mask e-girls, which led to me being recommended tradwife content and imagery similar to that on worth_fighting_for's Instagram. When I returned to my homepage, it had already been populated with recommendations of imagery from the girlblogging genre, including frequent pictures of baby deer, angels and pop cultural touchpoints such as *The Virgin Suicides*, *Lolita* and Lana Del Ray. However, it had also been recommended images I recognised from pro-anorexia (pro-ana) and eating disorder communities, namely shots of skeletal white women.

'It's definitely there', replies Woodrow, when I ask about the prevalence of #Thinspo content in communities of white nationalist teenage girls. 'What I worry about is the way that a person's capacity for critical thinking is totally kneecapped, by starvation and fasting.' Woodrow points out that this decrease in critical thinking could leave young women 'more vulnerable to being groomed'. 'Even if there's nobody at the top pulling the strings […] you have a subculture that values being super thin, and also being really young […] and those people are also sharing white nationalist propaganda. It doesn't seem like a huge leap to me to think that that is a population that would be especially vulnerable to that propaganda', she tells me.

Social media is enhancing a tactic that the alt-right and far right have been using for a while: employing women as the respectable, smiling faces of the movement to lure in a wider audience. 'All of these individuals are creating an on-ramp to radicalisation and making it exponentially easier for a young person at home to become radicalised', journalist Daniel Lombroso explained to me, adding that women are in many cases more effective propagandists than men in the movement. While creating his film *White Noise*, which follows the prominent far-right influencers Richard Spencer, Mike Cernovich and Lauren Southern, he noted that Southern was the most skilled propagandist of them all. For Lombroso, this might be explained by Southern's authenticity as well as her femininity, which allows her to 'walk the line between dog whistle white nationalism and out-and-out white nationalism'.

'The women who've really built viral followings are kind of untouchable in a way that Richard Spencer isn't [because] Richard Spencer is so laughably ridiculous', says Lombroso. 'He's so performative, no one in the movement likes him. But in a way, the women almost have a godlike status, even though Lauren [...] is filled with hypocrisy. She's filled with confusion. She almost expresses regret and then takes it back. [But] people love her. They want pictures with her. [...] She has immense pull.'

As we've seen, once they've engaged with these influencers on accessible platforms such as Instagram and YouTube, women can then make their way into 'dark socials' such as Telegram channels, WhatsApp groups or secure servers. 'One path is through the radicalisation ladder where they start off in fairly accessible – I don't want to say benign – less extreme online spaces that try to be a little bit edgy', researcher Emily Gorcenski explains. 'And then from there, it's really easy to follow the trails to the 8Chans or 8kuns to sites like Stormfront, to more radical right-wing content.' Women either 'lurk' in these communities, partake casually or, as Gorcenski puts it, hone their skills as propagandists and FFIs. 'We do see that women in online spaces do know how to wield influence over men', she tells me. 'We see this in gaming spaces, we see this in forums going back to the early days of the internet. That's not to say that they are respected and it's not to say that they are appreciated, but there are some women who have learned how to navigate the social dynamics of these spaces.'

5

What is a woman? Mapping women's radicalising content

Women and men can follow a similar process of online radicalisation: coming across forward-facing content such as memes, viral videos or discussions and following them to back-facing content such as blogs, web forums and Discord servers, where they are exposed to more extremist and radical content. As the authors of *Meme Wars* explain:

> One of the key ways that meme warriors suck people down into these rabbit holes is through the artful use of red pills ... provocative ideas that challenge the status quo, and which meme warriors might send out in tweets, or drop into a comment section, or call in to a radio show to plug. The hope is that you might be driving your car and hear one of these ideas ... [and] you'll be curious enough about what you just heard to look into it, following the path into the rabbit hole that your research will lead you down.[1]

But what are the pink pills, created specifically to entice women into these rabbit holes? In this chapter we explore some of the most salient topics women discuss in far-right communities or cite as being the source of their awakening.

Anti-feminism

In December of 2022, a new trend popped up on TikTok. The video that started it was nothing too out of the ordinary: a young white woman, most likely in her early twenties, documenting her day. 'A day in the life of … ' videos are generally popular on the platform; as of writing the hashtag has 13.4 billion views. Videos under the tag range from 'A day in the life of a Vogue fashion editor' to 'A day in the life of a solo traveller in Bali'. This particular video was of 'A day in the life of a stay at home girlfriend'.

Posted by Kendel Kay, the video (which had 725,900 views as of May 2023)[2] sparked weeks of debate across social media. Many argued that Kay was glorifying financial reliance on men without the legal protection of marriage, which can leave women more vulnerable to abuse. Others pointed out the video's thematic links to tradwife content. Although Kay's political affiliations are unclear, she does have 'feminine lifestyle' in her bio – possibly a nod to notions of 'traditional femininity' and women's role in the domestic sphere. In June of 2023, Kay wrote an article in *Newsweek* in which she said: 'There are a lot of people who have said my videos are "anti-feminist" and that my lifestyle is going backwards. But I feel that feminism exists so women can have a choice to do whatever they want – and I think it's amazing that I have that freedom. I don't believe I am pushing back women's rights in any way.'[3]

Regardless of Kay's intentions, the right and far right capitalised on the moment. Jennifer Mock's video of the 1950s housewife meeting a modern woman (discussed in Chapter 2) was posted during the backlash to Kay's original post. Both creators found a receptive audience in Gen Z and Millennials (the generations born in 1996–2010 and 1981–1996, respectively), 52 per cent and 53 per cent of whom say feminism has gone too far and now discriminates against men, according to research from King's College London.[4] Unsurprisingly, men were more likely to agree with this statement, with a gap of 14 per cent between men and women across the global average. That doesn't undermine or contradict the success of anti-feminist influencers in any way; most have a majority-male audience.

While anti-feminist content for and by men may focus on women's supposed inferiority, depravity and subhumanity ('By the time a girl hits 25 years old, any man who meets her will have to deal with a walk-in closet of emotional issues and hang-ups from being pumped and dumped as much as a 1930's brothel whore', Roosh V once wrote for Return of Kings), anti-feminist content targeted at women focuses more on how feminism has caused many of the ills facing women today by tricking them into giving up their natural place and duties. 'As for female empowerment, there's nothing that has made me feel more empowered in my life than supporting and being supported by a strong man', alt-right blogger Claudia Davenport told the *Economist* in 2017.[5]

In part, the lure of this brand of anti-feminism is the promise of being able to retreat into the safety of white womanhood; to be infantilised and therefore placed beyond the reach of responsibility or reproach; to be cared for economically; to be led mentally and spiritually, as biblical women such as Kristen Clark and Bethany Beal of Girl Defined espouse in their videos about marriage and submission. This type of anti-feminism has at its heart promises that have never been extended to women of colour: that you will not have to work, that you will be protected and praised simply by virtue of your femininity, that you are a divine being and a saviour of the nation by way of giving birth. Not only this, but as Miranda Christou, a Senior Fellow at the Centre for Analysis of the Radical Right argues, tradwives' nostalgia for a time before feminism stripped women of their femininity, natural role, protection and leisure is built around a moment in time that is inherently nationalist. She writes:

> Traditions are frozen moments in history arbitrarily chosen from the cultural repertoire as 'the' authentic expression of the national collective. Oftentimes these traditions are invented, as [the historian Eric] Hobsbawm argued. Appealing to the importance of maintaining 'tradition' is one of the ways in which nationalist rhetoric claims an essentialized and largely a-historical version of culture.[6]

Hajar Yazdiha, an Assistant Professor of Sociology at the University of Southern California, tells me over email that Black women are missing from the rise of traditional domesticity, particularly the way it has been performed on social media. Tradwife content is inherently white, as it rewards choices made by white women that would result in punishment for Black women. 'The great waves of white feminism have only perpetuated the deeply unequal system that attributes white and Black women's choices with vastly different meanings. In this new age of the "Opt-out generation," white women's choices to stay home and embody tradwife roles can be seen as a feminist statement, a demonstration of the breadth of choice feminism allows.' Meanwhile, she explains, Black women who have made similar choices are demonised. Beneath racialised accusation of laziness, moral corruption and regressive behaviours is the understanding that Black women will be punished if they try to step outside their 'place' in our racist society.

Yazdiha further says that white women have been seen as the protectors of the purity of the white race since as early as the eighteenth century. This granted them a powerful role in society, one that Black women's procreational capability was seen to undermine:

> These ideas are deeply embedded in culture, where the 'Cult of True Womanhood' means white women are viewed as innocent, virtuous, and domestic, with a sense of frailty that had to be protected at all cost. Black women have been constructed as the opposite of delicate white women whose role is to uphold white femininity by quite literally serving it, whether as domestic or manual workers.

It is also important to look at whose traditions are being centred by tradwives. As Koa Beck makes clear in *White Feminism*, domesticity and housewifery have only ever been the 'tradition' of white, middle-class, heterosexual women. Women of colour and Jewish and immigrant women were often expected to work outside the home, and even if they were homemakers they did not follow the isolationist and individualistic tradition of white housewives. Instead they used collective action and unionisation to agitate for change within their communities.[7]

If we're exploring what it means to be 'trad', it's worth exploring what it means to be a wife. In an article on tradwives for *Bustle* magazine, journalist Jo Piazza opens with an anecdote that during an argument with her husband over housework, she shouted 'I want a wife!' She then clarifies:

> Except wife was the wrong word. I didn't want a clone of me. I wanted a false nostalgic robot of a wife. I wanted June Cleaver. Betty Draper (without the drama). I wanted someone to silently cook and clean and care for the children while I focused on work. I wanted something that really only ever existed on television.[8]

Like other Marxist feminists before her, in her essay 'The Wife Glitch', feminist writer Jennifer Schaffer posits that being a wife, and by extension a woman, is not a function of gender but a class of labourer. A wife is not just a woman who is married but, in the heterosexual context and particularly in the fascist imagination, an unpaid reproductive labourer. She is the keeper of the house, the children and the husband. Schaffer explains that as industrial capitalism boomed, the state took less responsibility for care work, pushing it back into the private sphere, giving rise to a type of Victorian, feminine responsibility in the home. 'The twentieth century saw the rise of a "family wage" for the working class; families were expected to survive on the husband's work alone, further ensnaring women in unpaid care roles. Pre-sexual revolution, the labor of the twentieth-century wife served as a critical support structure for the male worker', she writes.[9]

In the contemporary far right, the role of the wife as a 'support structure' for the male worker is perhaps most clear in the idea of women as 'helpmeets' in biblical womanhood. In fundamentalist beliefs – such as those Clark and Beal preach – women are completely subservient to their fathers and, later, their husbands, who are given permission to use physical punishment (known as 'Christian domestic discipline') on their wives. Hazel Woodrow, a researcher at Anti-Hate Canada, notes that 'one of the most alarming aspects of the online aspiring tradwife milieu is the network's overlap with adult men seeking these Christian domestic discipline and/or overtly sexual BDSM relationships. The Canadian Anti-Hate Network found "traditional femininity" Instagram accounts belonging to girls as young as 12, who were being followed by people with these apparent intentions.'[10]

After consuming enough tradwife content – and I have consumed more than enough for one lifetime in the course of writing this book – you start to notice a conspicuous absence: the trad husbands. Or really any types of husbands at all. While some FFIs do share videos of or with their husbands – particularly if their spouses are prominent members of the movement – most tradwife videos tend to focus on the woman alone, talking to the camera and performing domestic tasks. On TikTok, these tasks are filmed as static shots (requiring a tripod set up), to make it appear as if the subject is just going about her day naturally and we, the viewer, are a fly on the wall. There are sometimes multiple camera angles, and a voice-over explaining what is being done. While we may see children's clothes or toys, or the physical clues of a husband, they are generally absent from the videos.

I believe there are generally two reasons for this. First, as was originally the case for Lauren Southern and Caitlin Huber (Mrs Midwest) when they first began making videos, it is because they simply do not have a husband or child. Despite preaching that it was a woman's job to settle down and make babies as soon as possible, neither woman was married or had children until their mid-twenties, something that they were both denigrated for by men in the movement. Second, as we have already touched on, tradwife content is not necessarily being made to inspire other women to join the movement but to appeal to men. Nothing ruins the fantasy that the beautiful blonde you're watching lovingly bake a Victoria sponge could be your wife quite like her actual man stepping into frame.

There have been multiple stories of female content creators, particularly Twitch streamers, losing followers or facing a backlash after mentioning their boyfriends.[11] It bursts the bubble of the parasocial relationship viewers develop with these content creators.

I suspect that some tradwife creators have noticed that their engagement or viewership dips when they mention or show their husband/boyfriend, which means a dip in earnings. We are told these domestic tasks are being performed for a husband but often, in actuality, they are being performed for the camera, which is a stand-in for us, the audience. There are rarely trad husbands in these videos because we are the trad husbands for whom bread is being baked, floors mopped and chickens fed. What this disembodying of the husband also does, arguably unintentionally, is remove the concept of being a wife from the context of being in relation to a husband and naturalise it as something a woman just is. With the other part of the dynamic absent, being a tradwife becomes an extension of womanhood itself: we are watching her perform domestic labour not necessarily for anyone's benefit but just because that is what a woman does.

Looking at what doesn't make the cut in these videos is also illuminating. Discussing the book *Momfluenced*, Sophie Lewis notes that it 'never mention[s] the extent to which the racial-class performance of western motherhood is predicated on "surrogate" labours that it makes invisible, nor even the exclusion of these "surrogates" from the feed'.[12] This criticism could also be made of the momfluencer and tradwife content itself. That's not to say that all influencers, and specifically the influencer Lewis is criticising here, are far right, but denizens of both communities seek to create a vision of effortless domesticity – of napping babies, time to bake, aesthetically pleasing workout gear – that erases the labour and support that takes place off camera. This includes setting up the camera and doing multiple takes, in some cases meaning the domestic labour is being performed for the benefit of the viewer instead of the husband or children. In doing so, FFIs seek to promote this vision of domesticity in contrast to the rat race of 'having it all', that is, working outside the home while raising a family.

Catherine Tebaldi, an ethnographic far-right researcher and linguist, calls this the 'promise of leisure time'. She tells me that the infrastructure of social media – the millions of dollars of technology necessary to produce and share such videos – is also carefully erased from the vision of 'off-grid life' promoted by wellness influencers. The fact that this content is nearly always monetised also goes unmentioned. After all, it becomes much harder to encourage other women to become tradwives and unpaid domestic labourers for the far right if you're honest about being a part-to-full-time content creator. In these videos, we may see women feeding their kids, picking vegetables or folding laundry, but we never see them setting up a camera, editing in multiple software packages or creating a content schedule.

Content creation is skilled, time-consuming work – the type tradwives claim to eschew. It's also interesting to contrast this erasure of support, whether domestic or financial, with that of far-right male influencers, for whom the visibility of female domestic labour in their life is paramount to the performance of dominant masculinity. Misogynistic social media personality Andrew Tate, for example, often has conventionally attractive women performing domestic labour in the background of his videos, sometimes making them do tasks such as erase whiteboards or clear up after him. While much discourse around tradwives has unpacked what is meant by 'tradition' in this context, far less attention has been paid to what it means to be a 'wife'. After all, several of the women who make tradwife content are not actually wives but girlfriends, including Kendel Kay. The discussion could benefit from more feminist, specifically queer and family abolitionist, critique of the role marriage continues to play in the oppression of women and entrenching of gender.

This current wave of reactionary anti-feminism can also be read as a revolt against the failings of liberal, mainstream white feminism, which conflates empowerment with wealth and power accumulation, as well as against the failings of neoliberalism and late stage capitalism, which promises an endless upwards trajectory of profit, expansion and quality of life. Despite being the most educated generation of women in history, young women today are facing fewer employment prospects, more debt than ever before, political instability and climate breakdown. Is it any wonder some are willing to trade in their liberty for the veneer of protection and domestic bliss?

In an essay for *Dissent* magazine, Zoe Hu posits the tradwife/stay-at-home-girlfriend movement is in part an agoraphobic retreat from the mass panic around the threat of patriarchal and sexual violence exposed by the #MeToo movement. Hu likens the movement to lesbian separatism, despite the obvious ideological conflict. 'The danger of tradlife', she writes, 'is that it permits women to acquiesce to the state's neglect of this sphere. In an increasingly expensive and antisocial world, tradwives forsake life with others for the lonely, constrictive spaces of bourgeois ownership.'[13] Through this lens, the tradwife movement and its offshoots could be seen as an attempt by (white) women to keep our end of the bargain in the social protection racket, after the violence the system relies on was exposed by the #MeToo movement. Perhaps, though, this is too generous. For many of these women, anti-feminism is about power over others under a system that benefits them in as many ways as it oppresses them.

Anti-immigration and Islamophobia

Far-right groups using anti-immigrant and Islamophobic rhetoric have seen a significant increase in membership since the early 2000s. As Joe Mulhall points out in his book *Drums in the Distance: Journeys into the Global Far Right*, groups in both the US and UK adopted anti-immigration and Islamophobia as their key rhetoric around the turn of the century. In Europe and the UK, this was somewhat of a strategic move, away from the open anti-blackness and antisemitism of the postwar and 1980s far-right waves and towards policies that were felt to be more palatable and popular at the ballet box. (It should be noted that while they are less outwardly anti-Black and antisemitic, that doesn't mean these aren't key to the far-right worldview.) 'The [BNP's] decision to change the focus of their racism towards a different community is nothing new for the British far right. [...] [A]s public hostility towards the arrival of non-white immigrant communities grew, large sections of the UK far right shifted their attacks onto the new arrivals', explains Mulhall.[14]

In the US, the reason is more clear-cut, with Islamophobia sweeping into mainstream politics in the wake of 9/11 and the start of the invasion of Iraq. As Mulhall also lays out, much of the contemporary far right in both countries has its roots in the counter-jihad movement of the early 2000s. The EDL and its successor, Britain First, can both trace their roots back to counter-jihad movements.[15] This was certainly one of the appeals to Lucy Brown, who we met in Chapter 4. 'So [I] just like, had a bit of a mental breakdown in part caring about the terrorism at the time of 2017', she tells me, indicating why she first started listening to alt-right podcasts on platforms such as Infowars. A few months later, she would reach out to Tommy Robinson to offer him her skills as a video editor.

For women, anti-immigration and Islamophobic rhetoric is often presented through the lens of femonationalism, which is rooted in the view that non-white immigrants and Muslim men – who are often portrayed as one and the same – are a threat to women, their rights and their safety. 'The modern-traditionalist far right presents itself as the real defenders of women *and* women's rights, against an alleged "Islamisation" of Europe', writes political scientist Cas Mudde. 'Its exponents spout an eclectic mix of traditional racist tropes – innocent white women brutalised by animalistic non-white men – with pseudo-liberal defences of gender equality and womens' rights.'[16]

In this way, the far right is able to position itself as the true defender of women, protecting them from the threat of (usually sexualised) violence from an outside force. 'No self-control or respect for [white] women', reads a post in the Traditional Britain Telegram group from 18 July 2023, above a link to an ITV News article headlined 'Man Who Raped 70-Year-Old Sexually Assaulted Schoolgirl Just Days Earlier'. It is an archetypal post in channels such as Traditional Britain, PA or Tommy Robinson News. In the year I spent monitoring these channels as my alter-ego Ava, I saw similar posts added almost daily. Often, there wouldn't even be a caption, just a link to a news story about sexual violence committed by men of colour. Four days prior to that post, Traditional Britain shared a link to a *Daily Mail* story about undercover police officers fining men for catcalling women, opining: 'Give it five years and you'll have to take a pocket full of consent forms to even speak to a woman on a night out.'

But the threat that immigrant and Muslim men are presented as posing is not limited to sexual violence. As researchers Prithvi Iyer and Shruti Jain write: 'Since women have traditionally held dispensable part-time positions or worked in the informal sector wherein job security is low and competition with immigrants for limited resources is high, their grievances against immigration found takers within the far-right.'[17] By positioning themselves as femonationalists, far-right organisations can also claim to defend women's access to resources such as employment, housing, benefits and healthcare that might otherwise be 'taken' by migrant men. '[D]id you know that all immigrants who entered the Netherlands between 1995 and 2019 collectively cost the country 400 billion euros, mainly due to "redistribution through the welfare state?"', reads a message cross-posted to the Telegram channel Feminazi on 4 July 2023.

There are a few things to unpick here. First, it is only official far-right political parties such as the Brothers of Italy and the French Nationalist Party that use employment in this way; other far-right movements, including the alt-right, identitarians and some white nationalist groups are more overt about their desire for women to leave the workforce and return to the domestic sphere. As political analyst Sophie Boulter notes, 'although anti-immigration policies are a common theme, fascism's female face takes many forms, depending on the nation. Nations with more progressive cultures are more receptive to selectively progressive rhetoric coming from a (white) woman of the far right. Others want no progressive policies at all, or any nod to feminism, from far-right female candidates.'[18]

It is also an exercise in benevolent sexism, subtly suggesting that in a competition for resources, be it employment, housing or, as the more accelerationist groups suggest, food, water and safety, men will always come out on top (some groups try to get around this by suggesting that the state favours immigrants over naturalised men and women, giving them an advantage). Therefore, having fewer outsider men to compete with not only benefits women but also means there are fewer outsider men that insider men (read white) must protect them from. Either way, the message is clear: women will be safer and better cared for if there are fewer migrant men.

This brings us back to the patriarchy as a protection racket, but it is a protection racket that many white women are happy to partake in. As Alison Phipps writes in *Me Not You*: 'White women are deeply, and often deliberately, complicit with white supremacist violence, and our complicity usually takes the form of victimhood that appeals to the punitive power of the state.' She goes on to note that 'the same white men who purport to protect us from the Others do reserve the right to abuse and kill us themselves'.[19] As explored in Chapter 4, the far right does not care about protecting women from sexual violence; instead they seek to weaponise that threat against minorities (notably men of colour and trans women), protecting their own monopoly on sexual violence against white women explicitly,and all women implicitly.

Anti-blackness and antisemitism

While twenty-first-century far-right political movements may have shifted their outward rhetoric away from anti-blackness and antisemitism towards Islamophobia and immigration, it would be inaccurate to suggest that those earlier bigotries are no longer core to these movements. Group leaders such as Tommy Robinson and PA's Sam Melia may no longer make public references to the 'Jews' or 'the Blacks' (even they're aware that this would be too alienating for the public and would hinder their community building efforts), but the digital far-right ecosystem brims with anti-Black and antisemitic memes, discussions, dog whistles and imagery.

Jewish people are usually presented as the masterminds behind the issues in women's lives that attract them to the movement. For example, so-called Jewish elites (sometimes just referred to as 'elites' or 'liberal elites') are identified as the beneficiaries of feminism, since women entering the workforce outside the home means they are also paying taxes to 'Jewish-controlled banks'. Shadowy Jewish figures are named as the masterminds behind birth control or abortion, as they are seen as the 'puppeteers' of the Great Replacement, lowering white birth rates in order to replace white people in minority world countries with migrants from majority world countries.

Antisemitism is also at the heart of the anti-vax movement that has surged in popularity since the beginning of the COVID-19 outbreak in 2020. To be clear, the anti-vax movement has existed for as long as vaccines have, but this most recent groundswell has acted as an antisemitic, wellness, anti-government and deeply conspiratorial pipeline, one that intermingles with QAnon to create a seemingly absurd blend of politics and beliefs. Like many conspiracy theories, the anti-vax movement claims, either explicitly or implicitly, that Jewish elites were behind the mandatory vaccine rollouts that took place in 2021. It's difficult to overstate the impact or the sheer number of people pursuing QAnon, conspiratorial or far-right rabbit holes.

Transphobia and anti-LGBTQ+

In 2021, the philosopher Judith Butler was interviewed by queer historian Jules Gleeson in the US *Guardian* about why '[w]e need to rethink the category of woman'. The two queer academics discussed the changing notion of womanhood and queer identities. In the original version of the piece, Butler referred to trans-exclusionary radical feminists (TERFs) as 'fascists', saying '[t]he anti-gender ideology is one of the dominant strains of fascism in our times'.[20] Unsurprisingly, despite Butler being one of the world's foremost voices in gender and feminist thought, the backlash was swift and vicious. Butler found themselves on the receiving end of vitriol for speaking out about gender. The *Guardian* caved to pressure and removed the line from the piece shortly afterwards, only acknowledging the removal by adding: 'This article was edited on 7 September 2021 to reflect developments which occurred after the interview took place.' The incident came to encapsulate the toxicity of the so-called gender debate, where major thinkers are censored by the press and harassed by 'anti-gender' activists.

Over the last decade, transphobia has become one of the most salient and effective methods of radicalising women. In an article for *Vox*, trans journalist Katy Burns explains that TERF and gender critical feminism 'opposes the self-definition of trans people, arguing that anyone born with a vagina is in its own oppressed sex class, while anyone born with a penis is automatically an oppressor. In a TERF world, gender is a system that exists solely to oppress women, which it does through the imposition of femininity on those assigned female at birth.'[21]

TERF was once a somewhat fringe belief, having grown – in part – out of the anti-sex and lesbian separatist camp of the feminist/lesbian sex wars.[22] It also has roots in the rational scepticism movement of the 1990s and early 2000s, which set out to debunk anything that was seen as 'junk science'. Now, it is a project of mostly cis, straight, middle-class white women – as evidenced by the demographic of the so-called LGB Alliance (LGBA), a British charity founded in 2019, which claims to 'prioritise the needs and rights of same-sex attracted people'. In actuality, the LGBA focuses its efforts entirely on attacking the rights of trans individuals.

Several writers have speculated that one of the reasons TERF and gender critical feminism has become so prominent in the UK, despite its American roots, is British feminism's overwhelming whiteness and links to imperialism and nationalism, such as those between the Suffragette movement and the BUF discussed in Chapter 2. As Sophie Lewis, author of *Abolish the Family: A Manifesto for Care and Liberation*, explains, in other parts of the world, mass movements in the 1990s, 2000s and 2010s around the impact of globalisation and police brutality resulted in a societal dialogue about race, gender and class. However, this dialogue was much more limited in the UK. 'As a result, middle- and upper-class white feminists have not received the pummelling from black and indigenous feminists that their American counterparts have, and thus, their perspectives retain a credibility and a level of influence in Britain that the Michigan Womyn's Festival could have only dreamed of.'[23]

With this in mind, it is perhaps unsurprising that the language of transphobia from the far right, as well as from TERFs and gender critical feminists, has come to mirror that of femonationalism, claiming that invaders (often portrayed as men) pose a threat to the safety of cis (white) women. This threat is frequently sexualised, as it is with immigrant men in far-right rhetoric. In the case of transphobia, the spaces posed as being under threat of invasion are not states but so-called women's spaces such as gender-segregated toilets, sports changing rooms, shelters and prisons. The last of these is telling of the ways in which TERFs aim to preserve a status quo that harms marginalised women for the benefit of privileged women. '[T]his is bourgeois feminism rooted in disdain for those who think and live differently, whose bodies are not easily assimilated to capitalist production and reproduction', writes Phipps in *Me Not You*, continuing: 'Reactionary feminism, like conservatism, is deeply ideological in its policing of "appropriate" gender and sex.'[24]

We can also interpret the gender critical movement as seeking to protect the borders of gender itself, which, despite marginalising cis (white) women, provides a sense of identity, community and, most importantly, power – over people of colour, immigrants, trans and queer people and children. Alyosxa Tudor, an associate professor at the Centre for Gender Studies at SOAS, suggests that the backlash against critical race theory, the decolonisation of the curriculum, BLM activism and 'the mere existence of trans people' blurs these movements together, presenting them as a deliberate attempt to hide the truth about history and biology. They write: 'It is through this backlash that it becomes evident, of course, there is no thinking about the question of what gender, or indeed, a woman, is without investigating the role of racism, colonialism, and nationalism for the emergence of gender.'[25]

Tudor frames TERFism as a 'white distraction', one which allows white cis women to focus not only their activism but also large amounts of attention and column inches to defending and enforcing a type of womanhood and gender binary that benefits only themselves and white cis men (and oppresses all women and gender minorities). In doing so, not only do they centre themselves in feminist thought, they also centre themselves in conversations about queer rights and bodily autonomy. (Often I have wondered what progress I and my feminist and queer siblings could be fighting for, if we weren't so preoccupied with defending rights won by our foremothers and predecessors.)

Koa Beck furthers Tudor's argument, describing white feminism (she includes trans-exclusionary and gender critical feminism under this banner) as an impulse not only to centre oneself in gendered oppression but also as a refusal to engage with the ways in which women can also be oppressors on the axis of gender. This includes having power over trans people, queer gender identities and indigenous and non-Western genders, as well as on the intersection of gender and race. Sophie Lewis also explicitly links TERF and gender critical movements to colonialism, noting: 'It's also worth noting that the obsession with supposed "biological realities" [...] is part of a long tradition of British feminism interacting with colonialism and empire.'[26]

Transphobia as a recruitment and radicalisation tactic for women also overlaps with the far right's natalism, veneration of mothers and oppression of children, most notably in how trans rights and liberation (and even existence) has been reframed as a threat to children and parental rights. The overlap of the two is telling of the far right's worldview regarding children. Like women, they view them not as worthy of protection because they are humans, and all humans are deserving of safety and dignity, but because they are property: first of their parents, then their father and ultimately their race/nation/God (depending on the subdivision of the far right in question). It is no coincidence that Mumsnet, originally a forum for parents, has become the site of choice for the British TERF and gender critical movement.

'Mumsnet is to British transphobia more like what 4Chan is to American fascism',[27] writes British journalist Edie Miller, referencing the website's forums and the way in which, much like 4Chan's /pol board, Mumsnet's Feminism subforum has become overrun with transphobic posts and discussions. Opening the forum on a typical day, you'll be met with post after post like 'Sex Matters video on TRA violence and letter to Rishi Sunak' and 'Suella Braverman statement about police behaviour and TRA [trans rights activists] police officer response'.[28] Rarely are there posts about issues facing women, such as cuts to social housing, the wage gap, medical misogyny/misogynoir (the intersection of misogyny and racism experienced by Black women) or lack of affordable childcare, unless these can be weaponised against trans individuals. In this way, gender fascists use women's rights as a cover to try to legitimise their bigotry, as opposed to actually fighting for women's liberation.

Researchers from Binghamton University, Boston University and University College London, as well as the SPLC, offered some of the first analyses of how communities that converge around these topics online interact with each other as well as with different digital communities. They mapped six online women's ideological spaces: mainstream feminists, gender critical feminists, female dating strategy, femcels, red pill women and women going their own way. They identified the last four as being analogous with manosphere communities, including pick-up artists, incels and MGTOW. Their research supports the idea that gender critical feminists have more overlap (in both ideology and user base) with groups analogous to the manosphere than with mainstream feminism. "r/GenderCritical [a gender critical subreddit] has more normalized user overlaps with 6 out of 8 Manosphere Analog subreddits compared to any of the Mainstream Feminist subreddits; this suggests an underlying relationship with GCFs [gender critical feminists] and some of the Manosphere Analogs," they write. Further, their research found that after trans people, gender critical feminists align with femcel communities in being most likely to direct attacks at ethnic minorities, particularly Muslims.[29]

Alex DiBranco of the IRMS points out that when we talk about women in the far right, we're overwhelmingly talking about cis women, and that the supremacy of cisgender people is another way in which they are being appealed to. She also explains to me that TERF and gender critical movements, like far-right movements, are male supremacist. 'When we refer to something like trans exclusionary radical feminists, we talk about them as male supremacists even though they self-define as feminists, because they are reinforcing biological essentialism and the tenets of male supremacism', she tells me.

In America, the link between transphobia and so-called parents' rights is exemplified by the use of the slur 'groomer' for trans and queer individuals, which was popularised, in part, by Chaya Raichik and Libs of TikTok. 'No person or entity has been more influential at inciting this hate than the anti-LGBTQ+ Twitter account Libs of TikTok', says the ADL, noting that 'Libs of TikTok essentially acts as a compass, guiding anti-LGBTQ+ activists towards targets for harassment and protest. Drag events, such as family-friendly drag shows and "drag queen story hours," have become a popular target for anti-LGBTQ+ activists, who believe such events "sexualize children" and are encouraging young people to embrace an "immoral lifestyle".'[30] This tactic has resulted in increasing violence and attacks on trans and queer rights, most notably in Florida, where Governor Ron DeSantis has passed multiple bills that aim to roll back LGBTQ+ rights, including the 'Don't Say Gay' bill and bans on gender-affirming healthcare.

By positioning queer people as groomers, the far right and gender fascists paint them as the ultimate 'other' – a sexualised threat to children. This is a tactic that has been successfully used against marginalised groups throughout history, notably immigrants and Jewish communities through the Blood Libel. It also played a crucial role in the Satanic Panic of the 1980s–1990s and the QAnon conspiracy, both of which centre on the belief that groups of paedophilic satanists are sacrificing children. In its more modern iterations, from the Satanic Panic onwards, it can be linked to the right's fear of women's increasing power and role outside of the home. By spreading propaganda that preschools and schools are unsafe for children because of either satanic paedophiles or teachers 'grooming' kids by hanging rainbow flags in their classrooms, the far right seeks to drive women back into the domestic sphere, returning to a model of childcare and schooling that takes place exclusively in the home.

'If women's entry into the workplace in the latter half of the 20th century triggered deep anxieties about the decay of traditional gender roles and the family unit, in the 21st century it was same-sex marriage, growing acceptance of transgender rights, and the seeming cultural hegemony of a social justice agenda', writes journalist Ali Breland in *Mother Jones*.[31] He draws a through line from the racial segregation of the Jim Crow period and fears about Black male virility to the modern-day 'bathroom bills', which are sold in part on the fear that predatory men might claim to be trans women in order to access women's bathrooms.

It's worth noting here that as early as 2014, Media Matters for America debunked the myth that allowing people to use the bathroom that matches their gender identity would lead to an increase in attacks on women and girls. They brought together experts from 12 states and found that the myth that men would lie about being trans to gain access to women's bathrooms was 'completely unsupported by years of evidence from states that already have non-discrimination laws on the books'.[32] They also found evidence of anti-LGBTQ+ groups fabricating stories of assaults in bathrooms which were then picked up by conservative and even mainstream news outlets. If nuclear families represent the safety of the nation state, anything that poses a risk to that unit, be it women's liberation, children's liberation, queerness or immigrant labour perceived as undercutting job security, is deemed a risk to the heart of the nation itself.

Back in Europe, another woman is at the forefront of attacks on queer rights in the name of 'the family' – Giorgia Meloni, Italy's first female Prime Minister and leader of the neo-fascist Fratelli d'Italia (Brothers of Italy) party. In January 2023, Meloni ordered state agencies to stop granting registrations to children born to same-sex couples. In July the party went further, ordering the cancellation and reissuing of 33 birth certificates belonging to the children of lesbian couples.

'We want a nation in which – whatever each person's legitimate choices and free inclinations may be – it is no longer a scandal to say we are all born from a man and a woman', Meloni said in a speech around the time letters were sent to same-sex mothers informing them that only the gestational mother would be included on their child's birth certificate.[33]

'For the far right, propping up male authority and promoting a nuclear family that sticks to the gender binary are central tenets of the broader nationalist project', Judith Butler explains in their censored conversation with the *Guardian*.[34] As if to exemplify this, Meloni said in a campaign speech: 'Yes to natural families, no to the LGBT lobby, yes to sexual identity, no to gender ideology, yes to the culture of life, no to the abyss of death.'[35] As with France's Le Pen, Meloni's womanhood acts as a cover for the violence of her rhetoric, allowing her to couch it in the language of family values.

'Terfs will not be part of the contemporary struggle against fascism, one that requires a coalition guided by struggles against racism, nationalism, xenophobia and carceral violence, one that is mindful of the high rates of femicide throughout the world, which include high rates of attacks on trans and genderqueer people', Butler said in that same interview with the *Guardian*.[36]

Anti-fatness and wellness

The far right hates fat people. Every far-right influencer has publicly identified fatness as a symptom and synonym for the decline of the West. To them, it represents slovenliness, greed and hedonism. Fitness and thinness (to the right, these are one and the same; they cannot conceive of a fat body being fit and healthy), on the other hand, represent attributes valued by the Christian work ethic, namely dedication and self-denial. The body also serves as a metaphor, the strength of men contrasted against the fragility of women.

Name a far-right influencer and they will have made content dedicated to anti-fatness. Abigail Shapiro (sister of right-wing commentator Ben Shapiro), who uses the moniker 'Classically Abby' online, posted a video in 2020 entitled 'The REAL Body Positivity: Adele looks fantastic – healthy is beautiful!' in which she argues that the body positive movement has gone too far and is now encouraging 'unhealthy' ideals. 'The thing that gets lost so often is that healthy is the key word. It's healthy body types. It's not all body types. All weights. It's healthy body types', she explains, implying that only certain body weights can be healthy.[37]

Caitlin Huber, known as Mrs Midwest, has a similar video, posted in 2019, entitled 'Let's Talk About Body Positivity … ' in which she also argues that 'it seems like that body positive movement has gone too far into positivity and what makes you feel good, than what it truly means to be positive towards your body'.[38] In both videos, the women position fatness as a signal that someone is lazy and 'neglecting to take care of their body', and present thinness/fitness as a moral imperative, one that is linked to self-denial and domination of the natural body. They also both explicitly link thinness to attractiveness, arguing that women should desire to be thin if they hope to attract a 'good man'. Once again for far-right influencers, women's worth and purpose is linked to their desirability to men and right-wing politics are positioned as a way for women to increase their attractiveness.

The right-wing writer Katherine Dee perhaps sums this up best in an article for *Unherd*: 'Ultimately, they're saying, "If it's Right-wing to be healthy, wouldn't you rather be Right-wing?" And honestly? Who in their right mind wouldn't vote for that?'[39]

Cat Tebaldi, who researches 'gendered digital traditionalism', suggests that body and food also serve as a way of 'habitualising' far-right politics, enmeshing it into the minutiae of people's daily routine, from the food and supplements they ingest, to the way they structure their days, to the types of exercise they do. 'It's never actually about good food. There's always some kind of gendered, racialized meaning assigned to it', she tells me, explaining that '[y]ou have to make it a practice because you have to do something with your time as this totally submissive housewife. You have to invest in [...] these daily practices which promote people's investment in these ideological structures, and then also promote the naturalisation of these ideological structures.'

If the role of a woman is to remain in the home, how can she re-entrench her far-right or white nationalist beliefs? Men can go off and fight and protest, but for women 'defending the motherland' is a much more domesticated activity. If they are the birthers of a nation, 'looking after their body' through ideologically driven wellness habits becomes a way to defend the white race. Tebaldi also notes that this type of consumption serves as a way to habitualise gender performance. This can be seen in many of the vlogs posted by female far-right influencers. Most follow the same style and structure as any other vlog by walking the viewer through the vlogger's day. But for FFIs, each choice made in their day (or at least each choice that makes it into the video – another conscious decision) serves to reinforce and promote their far-right views and way of life.

For example, 'day in the life of a stay-at-home wife/ girlfriend' videos may centre on housework, tending to crops/gardens/livestock, caring for children and partners and eating specific types of food that align with their beliefs, such as organic, raw or 'homegrown' (although as someone raised in a rural community, I tend to take claims of self-sustainability with a grain of salt). As the role of the mother is to both feed the children and pass down appropriate views to them, what food the children are given can be a way to combine these two roles. If she is a homegrown American patriot, this might mean brand-named American cuisine, or if she is a granola homesteader, she might opt for homemade, non-genetically modified produce. The end result is that food becomes an almost literal way to control your child's body and fill it with your beliefs.

The far right's body fascism is also rooted in white supremacy, specifically a fear of the Black body and sexuality. Sandra Strings, author of *Fearing the Black Body: The Racial Origins of Fat Phobia*, explained to *Daily KOS* that 'by the 18th century, race science was built out, expanded to include additional physical characteristics. To the extent that people were linking indulgence in the oral appetite to an animalistic inability to control oneself, fatness became linked to the racial group adjudged to lack the capacity for self-government: Black people.'[40]

Much has been written about masculinist body fascism and exercise groups and forums, including bodybuilding.com, out of which the sprouts of the manosphere grew. But there has been less exploration of women's relationship to food and their bodies and the potential this has for far-right recruitment. Despite some gains from the body positivity and body neutrality movement, there is still overwhelming societal pressure on women to have a certain type of thin or 'fit' (which usually just means thin) body. Young girls are still the most at risk of developing eating disorders. Promising young women that they will be thin and attractive if they join you, whether you're a dieting app, weight loss programme or political movement, will have sway. This messaging is overt in the far right, from memes depicting fat, disfigured 'feminists' in comparison to thin, conventionally attractive tradwives, to swathes of conventionally attractive, thin FFIs explaining how much happier, healthier and more feminine they've become since taking up a 'traditional lifestyle'.

Going further, researchers from the University of Southern California have likened eating disorders to a type of radicalisation. Using the 3N model of radicalisation (need, narrative, network), they examined how digital communities centred on eating disorders, such as pro-ana and thinspo communities, drive extreme behaviour, notably dangerously restrictive dieting and self-harm. Kristina Lerman and the other co-authors of the study write:

> Individuals experiencing body image concerns may feel devalued and rejected, and are therefore vulnerable to being radicalized. Loss of personal significance motivates them to restore it by seeking out meaning and identity from extremist communities. These communities also provide narratives that promote and justify extreme behaviours like food restriction, purging, or self-harm that restore personal significance, i.e. the thin ideal.[41]

Many of the most popular tradwife content creators and FFIs post content that overlaps with the types shared in eating disorder communities. For example, they post 'what I eat in a day'-style videos, wherein they often eat dangerously low amounts of calories. Part of the appeal of tradwife and FFIs is the fact that they are *thin and therefore seen as aspirational*, an aspect that has so far been mostly overlooked in discussion of them. As Hazel Woodrow found, young girls in eating disorder communities are often vulnerable to grooming and outside influence. We also need to understand this in the context of how prevalent eating disorders and dieting content is in young people's digital lives. The Center for Countering Digital Hate found that eating disorder content was served up on TikTok every eight minutes, and vulnerable accounts (such as those with 'loseweight' in their username) were served three times as much of this harmful content as others.[42] It is well established that bodybuilding and fitness content has been used to recruit men into the far right, yet the ways in which young women with eating disorders are vulnerable to far-right radicalisation or grooming has gone unexplored.

Abortion, contraception, natalism and motherhood

As this book has hopefully made clear by this point, the main reason the far right needs women is for their reproductive capacities. That reproductive labour can be secured in two ways: willingly or by force. While the men of the far right are open to either (and many actively advocate the latter), appealing to women on the former has been a successful recruiting tactic.

As Seyward Darby explores in *Sisters in Hate*, natalism and natural birthing has been an in-road for many women in various far-right and white nationalist movements. Darby notes that several online natural birthing communities have self-radicalised into far-right spaces.[43] Birth can be a hugely traumatic experience for many pregnant people. Despite medical advances, it's still life-threatening (most notably for Black women), agonising and invasive. Thanks to medical misogyny, there have been fewer advances in childbirth than other areas of healthcare. Traumatic birthing experiences can leave women with an understandable and deep mistrust of doctors and the medical establishment, and this has either been exploited intentionally or served as a catalyst event, leading them to seek out content about alternative forms of medicine (which then connects back to the health, wellness and anti-fatness pipelines) and conspiracy theories such as big pharma, anti-vax and QAnon. The COVID-19 pandemic led to a massive influx of anti-vaccine conspirituality, with women making up large proportions of these communities.

Anti-hormonal birth control is another pipeline that has been gaining traction in recent years, particularly among young women online. On TikTok, the hashtag #naturalcycles had 59,600 views as of December 2023, and mostly consists of young women discussing their 'hormone-free' journey of coming off contraception such as the pill or coil in favour of the 'family planning method'. The popularity of the term 'natural cycles' to discuss what is essentially the 'natural family planning' or 'fertility awareness' method has not come from nowhere; it was sparked in part by a rise in usership of the app Natural Cycles, which claims to be a '100 per cent hormone-free', 'zero side effects' alternative to the pill and other hormonal contraceptives such as the intrauterine system coil or implant. While Natural

Cycles claims to be 99 per cent effective if used correctly, there are many reports of accidental pregnancies as a result of using this method.[44]

In other videos, young women read off the litany of side effects associated with hormonal contraception or use their sheet of side effects as a blanket. As with most of the red pill topics women congregate around, there is a grain of sand buried deep in the pearl – the pill sucks. It is overprescribed, often with little consideration of circumstances, and it does come with a litany of side effects, which are under-researched and often flat-out denied by the medical establishment.[45] Woodrow, who was raised a traditional Catholic, says she is now seeing rhetoric similar to that taught to her as a child – for example that birth control causes breast cancer and infertility – proliferating among teenage girls online. She says:

> Now I'm hearing it from teenage girls who like look like my very normal sister on TikTok, and they're not Trads, they're not Evangelicals, they're just regular teenage girls being like, did you know that if you take the pill, you're never gonna get pregnant. The problem is that they're not wrong, [about it being] an inequitable system and that we have never put a real strong effort into getting cis men on any kind of contraceptives. ... At the same time, I'm really afraid they don't know whose rhetoric they are using.

Arguably, both the homebirth movement and anti-hormonal birth control content can be linked back to the wellness pipeline and medical misogyny. Why *should* women trust doctors and midwives? 'When it comes to healthcare', writes journalist Anna Byrne, 'women are second-class citizens. They have poorer access to healthcare, and receive incorrect or delayed diagnoses and less effective treatments than men. Despite living longer, the average woman spends nearly a quarter of her life in poor health compared with a fifth for men.'[46] To further this, in countries where healthcare is privatised, notably America, wellness has become a way to shift responsibility back on to the individual. In the US, this is systemised through workplace wellness schemes where, in some instances, employees' insurance benefits are tied to their weight. As healthcare continues to fail women, and in some cases be completely inaccessible, wellness and conspirituality offer a way to feel in control of your health and welfare outcomes.

This is not to excuse or even sympathise with those who push anti-vaccine and other harmful rhetoric via wellness communities, but if we are serious about addressing women's radicalisation, we must look at the systems at play in women's lives. It's also important to note the role of medical misogynoir. While vaccine hesitancy is high among people of colour and there are large numbers of people of colour in wellness and conspirituality communities, they are not contributing to far-right movements to the same degree as white women. Whiteness is an important factor to the conversation around wellness and radicalisation as misogyny. In *Nice White Ladies*, Jessie Daniels argues that this is because the wellness industry in its current form is itself a reflection of whiteness – not only in how it prioritises a type of health measured against white bodies but also in the way it encourages individualised solutions to what are systemic issues.[47]

In her book *Bodies under Siege: How the Far-Right Attack on Reproductive Rights Went Global*, Sian Norris lays out the ways anti-abortion movements move from digispheres to international politics, in a pipeline almost shadowing that of radicalisation.[48] Extremist beliefs about abortion fester in online communities, before finding footing in more mainstream digital spaces and allies in tradwife and anti-LGBTQ+ women. From there, these ideas are taken offline via conferences funded by far-right organisations and oligarchs. For example, the National Conservatism Conference, which in 2023 hosted anti-abortion speakers, is funded by the Edmund Burke Foundation.[49] Here, they get picked up by politicians, who take them back to their country's governments. '[The anti-abortion movement] is international, it is networked, and it relies on global wealth to carry its extremist ideology about women's bodies into the mainstream', Norris writes.[50]

Norris also notes how other movements, including those of TERFs and gender criticals, follow a similar process. Many of these groups, which on the surface are ideologically at odds, have formed coalitions of what researchers Kath Browne and Catherine J. Nash call 'heteroactivism',[51] aiming to re-establish the dominance and hierarchy of the heterosexual nuclear family. Browne and Nash outline how heteroactivists not only look to reinforce the supremacy of binary genders in law and policy but also seek to undermine LGBTQ+ and other progressive social policies via religious discrimination laws, free speech policies which support attacks on academic freedom and platforming speakers who attack trans rights.

To do this, the activists frame their opposition to trans and queer rights, abortion access and liberalising gender norms as a quest to protect parents' rights to teach their children their own beliefs. As a result, TERFs and anti-abortionists have become bedfellows with far-right organisations like CitizenGO and the Heritage Foundation in order to promote their worldview.

Climate denialism and eco-fascism

The climate denial movement is male supremacist. It is a movement fuelled by an economic system that glorifies exploitation and domination. 'Male reactionaries view climate activism and general care for the planet as the feminization of their world', writes Ecofeminist Assad Abderemane.[52] Research also suggests that men are more likely to resist environmental actions such as recycling, which they view as emasculating.[53] While on an individual scale this may manifest in small ways, such as men steering clear of green products or engaging in littering, on a larger political scale it can have devastating effects. A clear example is former president of Brazil Jair Bolsonaro, a dedicated male supremacist whose administration between 2019 and 2022 allowed the deforestation of the Amazon – the Earth's lungs – to soar to a 15-year high.[54]

Masculinist denial of climate change and the desire to resist sustainable policies and actions such as cutting global emissions can be seen as aligning with other anti-feminist aspects of the far right. While it might be tempting to compare women's alignment with climate denialism and their alignment to anti-feminism, I fear that this in itself might be an exercise in benevolent sexism – one that assumes women are more nurturing and attuned to the natural world and therefore not sympathetic to its domination. This is not necessarily the case. Such an argument overlooks the fact that climate denialism is a colonial and racist venture, one that Western nations and white people in particular benefit from. As environmental journalist Diyora Shadijanova writes: 'When people focus on overpopulation rather than examining unsustainable overconsumption by rich countries, they're deliberately ignoring the root causes of the climate crisis.'[55]

On the flipside of climate change denialism is ecofascism, an ideology that combines fascist ideas with environmentalism, or environmentalism that drifts towards fascistic beliefs. '[E]cofascism is any environmentalism that advocates or accepts violence and does so in a way that reinforces existing systems of inequality or targets certain people while leaving others untouched', explains University of Connecticut researcher Elaina Hancock.[56] Bernhard Forchtner, one of the authors of *Climate Obstruction: How Denial, Delay and Inaction Are Heating the Planet*, goes further by writing for *OpenDemocracy* that 'ecofascism can be understood as a radical blend of ethnonationalism and authoritarianism, rooted in a belief that the land and the people are symbiotically interwoven, and form an organic whole'.[57] The ideology is growing among the far right and has already resulted in real-world violence. Both the Christchurch and El Paso shooters reference eco-fascism in their manifestos, with the El Paso shooter explicitly referring to himself as an 'ethno-nationalist eco-fascist'.

The movement acknowledges the very real threat of the climate crisis but believes that it has Malthusian causes.[58] It therefore argues for nationalistic border protection or even eugenicist or genocidal solutions. On a more esoteric level, eco-fascism links the wellbeing, culture and survival of a race (often explicitly identified as white) inextricably to the land from which that race originates. This is evident in the slogan 'Blood and Soil' (*Blut und Boden*), which was used by the early Nazis to justify calls for the Aryan domination of Europe in the 1920s and 1930s.[59] In post-internet far-right movements, this line of thinking is often adopted by 'crunchy Nazis', or far-right movements that centre around Norse/Pagan mythology. For women, this is once again linked to their role as birthers of the nation or mother goddess archetypes, and as such overlaps with wellness, new-age/conspirituality and natalist pipelines and communities.

Anti-radicalisation, anti-fascist and counter-terrorist groups have been slow to identify and acknowledge the climate crisis and the 'debate' around it as a site of radicalisation, often admittedly so. As such, there is less writing on the issue compared to other pipelines such as anti-immigration or anti-LGBTQ+ sentiment. Given that there is a dearth of research (particularly academic) on women's radicalisation – although this is changing – there is very little available about women and eco-fascism/climate denialism. However, this does not mean it is not a threat.

That said, eco-fascism and climate denialism do intersect with women's pain-points and pipelines in some clear ways – natalism, birth control, and eco-fascism being a case in point. As Annabel Sowemimo, a doctor specialising in community sexual health and reproduction, notes in a piece for *Novara Media*, 'reproductive rights are becoming a key battleground for environmentalists today'. In the same piece she goes on to say:

> Aside from the evident neocolonialism of a few wealthy countries continuing to dictate the reproductive policy of some of the world's poorest; the idea that we must curtail population growth because of insufficient resources is a blatant denial of the real state of things. The resources have rarely been the issue; it's about who consumes them and how.[60]

Although the far right is often broadly painted as anti-abortion/birth control (which they often identify as one and the same) and pro-natalist, this is a generalisation. The far right is eugenicist towards people of colour and disabled people, while advocating for forced birthing/motherhood for white announced female at birth people. In far-right spaces it isn't uncommon to see memes about welfare queens (an anti-Black stereotype that poor Black women have multiple children in order to be entitled to more welfare) nestled among discussions of falling white birth rates and how the pill has led to the degeneracy of white women.

The thing the majority of these pipelines have in common is bodily autonomy: the autonomy of announced female at birth people over their sexuality, reproductive system and overall health and wellbeing; the bodily autonomy of queer, particularly trans, people and their capacity to access healthcare, surrogacy and sexuality; the bodily autonomy of children to be free to learn about their body, sexuality and gender without being exploited. For the far-right to control the state through authoritarianism, it must control the bodies of its men: they must be fit, strong and healthy for the (unending) war against invaders. They must be able, willing and keen to reproduce in state-sanctioned, white, heterosexual family units. And their bodies must exist in a strict hierarchy, white over non-white, male over female, adult over children, 'abled' (if such a thing exists) over disabled, and on and on. Anyone whose body falls too far outside the safety of whiteness, heterosexuality, cisness and naturalised identities is a danger, an invader, a groomer, a rapist, a cancer, a pervert, unnatural, threatening, sick, danger, danger, *danger*.

As we've seen, women are attracted to far-right digispheres via a variety of content, some of which overlaps with that which appeals to men, including white supremacy, anti-immigration, antisemitism and so-called anti-gender-focused discourses. However, even within these topics, FFIs and radicalised women tend to focus on the way women are affected, for example by framing anti-immigration content through a femonationalist lens. Women also tend to collect around radicalising content which exploits grievances specific to women, such as conversations around birth control or natural birth. Once women have begun interacting with these topics on a surface level, they are then funnelled towards more radical conversations and conspiracy theories via both algorithmic suggestions and communal prompts. But what happens to these women once they have been sucked into radicalised communities?

6

WHITE SHARIA NOW:
women's experiences in far-right communities

'It's like being trafficked in a lot of ways', Hazel Woodrow of the Canadian Anti-Hate Network explains to me, as we talk over Zoom about the radicalisation of young women into the far right. 'I think that effective models for deradicalisation and care afterwards could potentially lie at a nexus of what we know about cult recovery, gang recovery and trafficking recovery, because at the core of that is the feeling of "I have both been harmed and perpetrated harm".'

Through my years of researching women and radicalisation, the question of intention has been an itch I couldn't satisfyingly scratch. How deliberate is all this? Is the recruiting of women into this movement planned, discussed and executed in the way it is for young men, where Discord servers, channels and groups exist to infiltrate spaces where young men converge online and flood them with propaganda? Certainly, there are discussions about how to make the movement more appealing to women, or to bring more women onboard. But these discussions don't seem as organised or proactive as the drive to bring aboard men, a drive that has, for example, spawned an international ring of 'fascist fitness' groups designed to radicalise young men into combat readiness for the forever war of fascist thought architecture.

Or were the thousands of women striding across the periphery of these movements an unintentional bonus as they targeted men and boys? Woodrow's points provide some answers: women are predominantly recruited into the far right via their male spouses or by communities of other women. Reframing women's journey into the far right as trafficking allows us to account for the huge amounts of violence and harassment these women experience from within the communities. It also allows us to consider female far-right influencers and propagandists such as Ayla Stewart (Wife with a Purpose), Bethany Beal and Kristen Clark (Girl Defined), and Brittany Pettibone as traffickers: women who bring other women into the fold despite being aware of the harm that will come of it. Whether they do so for ideological reasons or perhaps to deflect harassment away from themselves becomes less relevant than the fact that they do it. As Woodrow points out, the fact that women in these movements are harmed does not diminish or excuse the harm they commit. The binary that victims cannot be aggressors and aggressors cannot be victims is one best left to the far right (and eventually destroyed, along with their movement).

Women in the far right commit great amounts of harm, to marginalised communities and to each other, but they are also on the receiving end of the movement's misogyny. White women have always played crucial roles in upholding white supremacy and held white supremacist views independent of men. As Ashley Mattheis, who has written extensively on extremism, notes, 'women's participation in organized racism and hate movements is an active, personal choice they make and not forced through coercion by the men in their lives'.[1] Women often join these movements fully aware of the harassment they will face from men. In this chapter, we explore the ways women are treated within far-right movements in order to better understand their experiences and see why many are willing to tolerate misogyny and violence in order to align themselves with white supremacy. We also consider what deradicalisation or methods for exiting these movements looks like for women.

Far-right misogyny

Extremist circles, instead of being at odds with dominant culture – as suggested by the frequent claim that extremists are a 'threat to our way of life' – are magnifying glasses of it. The beliefs of far-right extremists are not cooked up from nothing in Reddit forums, Telegrams channels, the backrooms of pubs, bedrooms and wherever else extremism festers. Their roots are deep in the soil of our society. While far-right communities actively work to shift the Overton window to the right, they can also be conceptualised as policing the borders (sometimes literally) of Western culture. The misogyny present in far-right and incel communities is often not that far removed from the kind we see in 'mainstream' online spaces (I only tentatively separate the two, which we discuss in Chapter 7), films, television and music.

'One of the benefits of studying extremist movements is that it gives you a reflection of society in its purest form. So there is always a nugget of truth that you find', journalist Daniel Lombroso tells me in our interview. For example, when people such as Richard Spencer say that everyone really knows America is a white man's country and needs to be kept that way, while no one else might say it so overtly, '40% of this country may believe that at some subconscious level'. Lombroso, who spent a year shadowing Lauren Southern for his documentary *White Noise*, believes the same can be said of people's opinions about women. 'Of course you meet the average corporate man, and he's never going to say, "I want my wife to have a career, but also to raise kids, but also to clean the house", but they show it in their actions.'

Like several other prominent female faces of the alt and far right, Southern has been pulling away from the movement over the last few years. Perhaps partly because the movement itself no longer offers the power and revenue it did in its heyday, but also because of the treatment she's received from her male colleagues. Southern, who rocketed to fame in the movement at its height when she was only a teenager, was on the receiving end of some of its worst exploitation of female far-right influencers. She has spoken publicly about being harassed for not having had children by her early twenties, as well as experiencing sexual harassment both on and offline. 'She came into this bright eyed and bushy tailed, and she realised over time that things were much, much darker than she ever expected', says Lombroso. 'When she says darker, she's referring to the opportunistic people who were using her fame to get famous and people who were ripping her off. But the principal thing she's referring to is the sexual violence and the sexual harassment.'

In 2024, Southern spoke to the right-wing news outlet *Unherd* about the abuse she experienced in her marriage, which ultimately broke down. 'I had this delusional view of relationships: that only women could be the ones that make or break them, and men can do no wrong.'[2] She went on to explain that no matter how she tried to appease her husband, his treatment of her only worsened, including calling her names, disappearing for days at a time if she disagreed with him and locking her out of her house with their small child. 'It was very strange, to go from being this public figure on stage with people clapping, to the girl crying, knocking on someone's door with no home to get into, being abandoned with a baby.'[3] Despite saying she was misled by an ideology that told her that only women cause relationships to fail by not being submissive, agreeable or feminine enough, she could not seem to bring herself to distance herself from the far right and red pill politics entirely. As of writing, she is once again actively posting on social media, including creating videos calling the mass graves of indigenous people discovered in Canada a 'hoax'.

While the far right presents itself as the defender of white women against foreign invaders and degeneracy, sexual harassment and violence is rife within its ranks. A 2021 article by the SPLC notes that '[a]necdotes of abuse abound, from white nationalist Richard Spencer being accused of emotional and physical abuse in 2018 divorce filings to allegations that Stewart Rhodes – founder of the anti-government Oath Keepers – engaged in emotional and manipulative abuse aimed at limiting his family's freedoms'. The article continues:

> These harmful acts, if true, are the physical embodiment of violent rhetoric and narratives from groups like the Proud Boys, who claim, 'leftist women are more third-wave feminist and less feminine than ever and now, you're not even women anymore ... either your women, and if you are, please stop fighting men, or you're not women and your face is now punchable'.[4]

This kind of rhetoric makes overt the violence in how gender is policed within these communities. Women must earn protection from men through correctly performing femininity, a core part of which, to these communities, is submission. 'That women like Lokteff, Southern, and Stewart can obtain and project power, influence, and social prestige in their roles as white power Barbies and tradwives reveals the source of tension', writes Tracy Llanera, co-author of the book

A Defence of Nihilism. 'In the alt-right, the success that women propagandists enjoy is tolerated because of its instrumental value, and if they (appear to) over-reach, they get punished. Their punishment, naturally, is coded in terms of their failure to fulfil their primary obligation as racist white women: to serve white men and the white cause.'[5]

Llanera posits that far-right women experience a unique sort of misogyny within these communities, one where the better they align with the movement's aims, the more they are punished for their failure as women. Any hint of gender non-conformity results in them being stripped of both their protection and their humanity.[6] That these men are protecting their women, or at least the ones that behave, from men themselves is only addressed insofar as it can be used to demonise men of colour (and increasingly, trans women and drag queens, whom the right views as men).

As with their other types of hate speech, these misog-ynists often hide behind a veneer of irony or trolling to shield themselves when they're called out and to help them mainstream their rhetoric. For instance, in an April 2021 livestream, far-right commentator Nick Fuentes told a viewer who asked how to 'punish' his wife for 'getting out of line': 'Why don't you smack her across the face? Why don't you give her a vicious and forceful backhanded slap with your knuckles right across her face – disrespectfully – and make it hurt?' He followed up later in the stream by saying: 'No, I'm kidding, of course. Just kidding. Just a joke.' But it isn't a joke. Intimate partner violence is something people live with every day. Even with the cover or irony, Fuentes is still minimising this behaviour, despite the fact that three female intimate gendered killings occur per day in America,[7] and two women per week are killed by their partners in England and Wales alone.[8] And of course, if this is what these men will say in public, we can only imagine what they say and do off camera.

Eviane Leidig explains to me that while these men do support female far-right influencers to a certain degree, this is often overshadowed by their misogyny. 'Even just on a live chat, for example, I would see comments from men degrading these women, and the way that they respond to these incidents is they'll just say such behaviour will not be tolerated on the platform and these men will get kicked off, or they'll just try to emasculate these male commentators', she says. She adds that the FFIs themselves don't acknowledge the stream of sexism directed at them. This was certainly true for Lucy Brown, Tommy Robinson's former PA, who tells me she eventually realised women 'were never seen as a person' by men in the far right, something she could not admit while still in the movement. She says the movement has left her with 'two stalking cases and like 10 grand down because you try to defend yourself against vexatious court cases with PTSD [post-traumatic stress disorder]'. Brown also experienced sexual harassment continuously during her time in the movement.

Far-right groomers

Grooming and abuse is also rife within far-right communities. Jake Hanrahan, a journalist who spent several years investigating the far right, has seen the violent ways this misogyny plays out even within their own ranks, and notes that the further right a group is, the more vile their treatment of women. Where alt-right groups may treat women as sex objects and advocate for the removal of their rights and autonomy, neo-Nazi's misogyny tends to be much more violent. 'That's more like "all women are just objects and we will treat them as such and if they want to be treated any other way, then they're useless and they should be killed". It's very dark', Hanrahan tells me. While he was investigating a self-described 'cultist, nihilistic neo-Nazi group', he found that they would often convince young teenage girls to record themselves self-harming and send videos to the members. 'They would just share it with each other, laughing about it "like, look what we made her do". A lot of them were also paedophiles, like openly, and they were talking about sharing paedophilic images with each other. They degraded [these girls] to the point where they entered levels of actually doing abuse. Just to kind of have a laugh at these girl's expense. It was fucking the worst thing I've ever seen, to be honest', he says.

Here, we can clearly see Woodrow's point that girls and young women are trafficked into the movement. While few women are brought into any alt- or far-right movement for their brains and skills, those targeted by more extreme far-right and neo-Nazi communities are explicitly recruited as sex objects to be exploited. Speaking about masked e-girls, as well as self-radicalising communities of teen girls and young women online, Woodrow also notes how they recreate the harassment, bullying and violence they experience from men among themselves. Groups of white nationalist, far-right or neo-Nazi girls will recreate the kind of intergroup bullying and gatekeeping often found among teenagers, but instead of ostracising one another for not keeping up with latest trends or knowing the most niche bands they will bully one another for not being extreme enough in their bigoted beliefs. 'They are incredibly cruel, internally and laterally, as well as being violent and inciting hatred and violence towards marginalised groups', says Woodrow. But this isn't the only kind of violence these young women are directing at one another; as well as luring other young women into groups where they will be sexually exploited by men, Woodrow says she has seen women and girls sexually exploiting and abusing one another.

Women who leave

Several women who have left the alt-right and far right have now spoken out about the abuse they faced while in it. For example, a woman who identified herself only as Samantha described some of the abuse she faced during the two years she spent in Identity

Europa, during which time she helped to organise the first Charlottesville rally. CNN explains in an article about Samantha:

> Even as Samantha thought she was rising through the ranks, she was aware of a meme known as white sharia, a misogynistic twist on Muslim religious code. The 'joke' is that white women are ruining Western civilization through promiscuity and voting for liberals, so the only way to save it is to impose Sharia law on women and, in the supremacists' twisted view of Sharia, treat them like property. A flyer at the book-burning said 'WHITE SHARIA ZONE. THOTS MUST WEAR HIJAB AT ALL TIMES'.[9]

Eviane Leidig explains that 'thot' (often described as standing for 'that hoe over there') is a common term for women in these communities, used particularly to dismiss tradwives by calling them 'tradthots'. The 'tradthot' has itself become an archetypal meme within online far-right spaces, and memes degrading self-professed 'traditional' women are common. Memes showing wojaks in tradwife-style garb, with annotations such as 'body count over 30', or showing a white woman cradling a mixed-race child, are regularly posted in Telegram channels with captions like 'here's your tradwife sir'. One such example, posted in the Telegram channel Femoids Unleashed, depicts a 'fat' blonde woman in a revealing outfit with the annotations 'body count 30' and 'Used up hole'. Beside her, it shows the same woman in the stereotypical tradwife outfit holding a Bible. The captions around her now read 'Bodycount 30 + dress + bible' and 'Used up hole with bible'. The message is this: no matter how much women dedicate themselves to the far right, they will only ever be sluts in the eyes of its men. 'There really is not any type of acknowledgement by these female influencers about the constant stream of messaging and sexism that's directed against them', says Leidig. 'But the irony is that any successful movement does need women behind it to propel it and to normalise it.'

In the same CNN article, another anonymous defector shares her boyfriend's views and the way the alt-right treats women in general:

> 'Women deserve to be subjugated. Women deserve to be humiliated. Women deserve to be raped. Women deserve to be impregnated.' It wasn't a joke. ... I can't believe I supported that stuff. I thought I was trash, so I didn't mind when they talked about women being dogs, worthless. Even though I was the one driving them around, paying for stuff. Like 70 percent of the time, the women earn the money and the men do podcasts. And they do podcasts about how women shouldn't have jobs.[10]

As we've seen, it's not just men preaching into Røde mics that women should return to the domestic sphere; several female influencers have now made forays into the right-wing podcast industrial complex. Dubbed 'the female Andrew Tate', Hannah Pearl Davis, known online as Just Pearly Things, has made a name for herself by promoting a worldview that women shouldn't vote or be able to work. Davis, who is clearly astute at content syndication and social media marketing, saw her following increase by 50 per cent following Tate's arrest, according to *Insider*. Across her platform she shares snappy, anti-feminist soundbites such as 'Women should not vote – Repeal the 19th!!!'[11]

Women who can't leave

Once they've reached the upper echelons of these movements, young women quickly become isolated from the outside world, making them even more vulnerable to abuse from the men within these communities. Radicalised people often become estranged from their family and friends and are shunned (understandably so) from normal society. A few women on the alt-right have vocally lamented how the men who talk a big game about protecting women have left them exposed to the backlash of their hateful views. In 2017, white nationalist Tara McCarthy took to Twitter to complain that '[m]en in the Alt Right are going to have to decide whether they will continue to passively/actively endorse this behavior, or speak out against it. If you want more women speaking publicly about ethno nationalism [*sic*], I suggest you choose the latter'. She rounded off the thread by saying: 'The problem I'm stating here is not that "there are trolls on the internet" but that people who proclaim to be on our side are trying to tear down women in our in-group. If you can't see why this is dysfunctional, I can't help you.'

On top of becoming isolated and reliant on the community once they're in it, many women who are drawn into extremism come from vulnerable situations and see the community as a solution or safety-net. In her book *Sisters in Hate*, Seyward Darby describes these kinds of people as 'seekers'. 'Anyone who joins the hate movement is a seeker to some degree, and maybe there are circumstances that make them particularly primed to be recruited. They're seeking something in that moment – maybe it's power, maybe it's meaning, maybe it's money because they see a potential profit in running a subscription-based platform.'[12]

Of course, just because some of these women come from vulnerable backgrounds and experience violence or harassment doesn't mean they shouldn't be held accountable for their actions. Marginalised people are more likely to be in vulnerable situations, such as active addiction, homelessness, abusive relationships or living in poverty, and the actions of the far right puts these people in further danger. But a victim mentality is at the very core of the alt-right's and far right's ideology. If it wasn't, it would be impossible for them not to see the ways in which white, Christian, cisgender, heterosexual, able-bodied people are elevated at the expense of people of colour, queer people, disabled people, Jewish people, Muslims, Gypsy, Roma and Travellers.

As Leidig points out as well, it's not just for supposed safety or community that women seek out the far right. For some, it's power or money. For others, it's the sense of agency and empowerment that they believe these movements can offer them. However, that power is centred around a woman's primary duty as a mother and wife. 'They are literally the reproducers of the nation', she tells me. 'So I won't deny that for an average woman who's attracted to the promise of having a voice and being visible, this is an opportunity for her to do so. Of course, that comes with certain restrictions, certain parameters on what shade she can offer.' Leidig goes on to explain that very rarely are women actually in leadership positions within the movement. At the same time, many of these FFIs are literally profiting off evangelising the ideology that women should be subservient homemakers.

Why women leave

There is very little research conducted into why women leave far-right or white nationalist movements. Perhaps this is to be expected, given how little overall attention is paid to women in far-right movements overall. Despite the mass of academic and journalistic flotsam that surrounds the far right, there is a lack of attention paid to the women who leave and their stories, particularly in comparison to the effort put into deradicalising and rehabilitating the men of the movement. One of the few academic explorations available, a report published by the University of Oslo's Center for Research on Extremism, found that for women, leaving is a three-step process, which involves 'becoming disillusioned, finding it imaginable to leave, and seeing life on the outside as possible'.[13] Notably, the report found that women did not leave because of the violence and harassment they experienced themselves, or because of the violence and harassment they participated in. Instead, they left when violence was directed at their children.

'Women whose children became involved in violence inside or outside the group left, as did women whose children were the targets of physical or sexual violence. In other words, women left when leaving seemed imaginable and staying became unimaginable', reads the report.[14] Seyward Darby's *Sisters in Hate* provides an example of this, detailing how white nationalist Corinna Olsen finally broke free of the movement – after several attempts – when men began to make sexual remarks about and to her young daughter. 'People don't leave the hate movement because a veil lifts and they are suddenly able to see hate for what it is', writes Darby, in a related article published by the *New York Times*:

> The truth is more disappointing. They leave because it makes sense for them, because the value hate once gave them has diminished or evaporated. Ms. Olsen seemed to know this, writing once on a blog, 'The reality is, people rarely change their personality or ideals during adulthood, and if they do, it needs to be something they do on their own, for themselves.'[15]

For many women, disillusionment came not because they started to see the world in a more nuanced way but because of conflict with other members, particularly with other female members, whom they rely on for community. 'It isn't surprising that problems with other members would sour women on far-right groups', notes the article published by the Center for Research on Extremism, 'since almost 40% of them came into right-wing extremism hoping to find a healthy and welcoming family that could substitute for the troubled relationships they had on the outside'.[16] However, the researchers also found that the fear created within these communities in order to breed distrust of the outside world can be shattered by personal experiences. 'Women left after they met someone on the outside who became a friend. Or when they took a social science course at a local college that opened their eyes to a different interpretation of society. Or when they got to know someone who was Jewish, gay, or African American.'[17] In a way, these experiences function as a 'blue pill' moment, a catalyst event destabilising their radicalised worldview and leading them to seek out more information that challenges the narrative of their community group.

Making life on the outside seem possible is also a crucial step in the process and one, in my opinion, that deradicalisation organisations are failing to acknowledge will look different for men and women. While both men and women need to feel there will be community awaiting them on the other side, as well as the possibility of work, for women the considerations may seem all too mundane: what good is it if a woman turns her back on her white nationalist beliefs if she and her children will be homeless if she leaves her

Make America Great Again hat-wearing, gun-toting husband? How can she 'leave' white nationalism if there is nowhere for her to go or, even if there is, she has no money to get there? Particularly, we must keep in mind the gender roles and relationships promoted in these communities, where a woman must be 'taken in hand' by her husband, who acts as the master of the house, including their finances. While FFIs may have lucrative careers as content creators, the same cannot necessarily be said for women in the movement who shy away from the camera.

We must also think of the increasing number of young women claiming that they are turning away from feminism and desire a 'traditional relationship'. What will happen to Instagram's homesteaders and TikTok's stay-at-home girlfriends when #TraditionalWomanhood is no longer trendy? There are already examples of this happening: Bella Greenlee, who used to make content sharing her life as a stay-at-home girlfriend, later spoke about the life, warning other women about the vulnerable position being financially dependent on her boyfriend left her in. 'If you give a man the power to feed you, he also has the power to starve you', she told *Cosmopolitan*.[18]

To be clear, this is not a call to see these women as nothing more than victims. As I discussed in Chapter 5, I believe it is both possible and paramount to be able to recognise that they are overwhelmingly survivors of intimate partner, sexualised and gender-based violence while still holding them accountable for the harm they have caused to marginalised communities. Ultimately, female formers pose tough questions for us as a society. Some will be fleeing domestic violence, but how can we ask other vulnerable women, particularly disabled, non-white, refugee and trans women, all of whom face disproportionate rates of sexualised violence, to share a space with women who could pose a threat to them? And is this question purely hypothetical, given the number of shelters that have closed in recent years? Who would fund a shelter for former neo-Nazis? Being asked to recognise that women can both be oppressed on the basis of their gender and oppressors on other axes such as race, settler status or cisness is something that acted as a catalyst event for many of the women we have met in this book, particularly gender critical and white nationalist women. So, if we are serious about addressing women's radicalisation, it is a topic we cannot shy away from.

7

Which way Western woman? Addressing the future of women in the far right

Radicalisation, particularly radicalisation that takes place primarily online, is generally conceptualised as a 'pipeline'. But during the years I have spent researching far-right radicalisation for this book, I have come to think of it as more like an ocean. Pipelines suggest that something is contained, and that it flows in one direction. Instead, the far-right's recruitment tactics are opportunistic: they take the shape of whatever situation they're in, whether that's a pandemic, an economic crisis or a new subculture or technology. Pipelines suggest an opening that you stumble across or walk into, but you can stride boldly into the ocean, or you can dip your feet in, out of curiosity, before looking back and realising you've drifted much further out than you thought; perhaps further than you can swim back. You can also stand at the shoreline, where the sea meets the sand, and watch as the waters wash around your feet, then ankles, then knees, and refuse to retreat.

Most importantly though, the ocean doesn't just take – it gives. It negotiates with the shore, it is beaten back and rises again. It regurgitates things from its deep, dark places. Shiny, curious ideas, scattered in the sunlight, which all of us, even those who would never think about going in the water, pick up and pop in our pocket, carrying them with us through the world even if we don't fully understand them.

In this final chapter, we explore how far-right beliefs have become more mainstream in the years since the COVID-19 pandemic and 6 January insurrection, what is driving this, and how we can begin to address the issue of women' involvement in helping to normalise these beliefs through their role as propagandists and organisers.

Support for far-right and populist politics is still rising, particularly in the UK, Europe and America. QAnon is gaining ground rapidly, even in mainstream politics, and two years of isolation and financial devastation has pushed many people down the dark path towards extremist communities. In late 2020, when I started making *The Feminine Art of Radicalisation*, the podcast that spawned this book, I wondered if it might feel dated by time it came out. Trump had just been voted out of office, taking the last dregs of the alt-right with him. In fact, when I interviewed Daniel Lombroso on the afternoon of 6 January, we joked about how we expected the formalisation of Joe Biden's victory to pass without much notice. That evening, I watched on the BBC as far-right protesters, QAnon adherents and Trump supporters stormed the Capitol Building. Despite this, Biden was sworn in. Trump was later indicted, and more than 1,000 people were arrested in connection with the violence of that morning.

'I don't think most people also know that in the lead up to the insurrection, there were a number of Trump rallies that were held across the US, and this was all organised by an organisation called Women for Trump', said Eviane Leidig in the original interview we did for the podcast. 'So again, I think it's so important for people to understand the role that women can play in these movements.' She went on to suggest that with Trump out of office – we spoke originally shortly after 6 January – the shock and the vacuum left within right-wing and conspiracy movements by his departure could lead to groups becoming more radical in the face of their disillusionment. 'The next big far-right leader, for lack of a better term, is going to be somebody who is really the opposite of Trump. I think we're going to see somebody who's very well-spoken, who's very articulate, educated and is able to really normalise and legitimise far-right narratives in a way that was so different from Trump's brashness and aggressiveness', she added. She noted that women could play a key role in legitimising this kind of clean-cut leader.

Leidig wasn't the only person who brought up the possibility of another right-wing populist rising to power and mobilising a similarly devout, far-right fanbase – but this time with more competence and establishment backing. In fact, several of my interviewees brought it up. 'Trump has created a space, but the far right has given him the space to say the most defamatory, disgusting racist, sexist things, and to get away with it', said Lombroso. He went on to say that parts of the far right might 'go into hiding', coming back out when the next populist leader begins to rise to power.

A worrying trend that has emerged since the bottom fell out of the alt-right is previous devotees of the movement drifting into other, possibly more dangerous communities such as QAnon or underground neo-Nazi groups. 'It's peaks and troughs', says Jake Hanrahan, explaining that one of the last periods of right-wing militancy was in the 1990s, before it died off some-what in the early 2000s and 2010s (in fact, some schol-ars suggest there have been five waves of the far right). 'Maybe these lads will realise "okay, there's a certain level of stuff we can get away with and we won't go to prison". They will adapt and give it a year or two. They'll have adapted it into a space where they start up again. It's just a constant battle. We just have to hope that enough people pay attention.'

We're already seeing this process happening with groups such as the Proud Boys in the fallout from the 6 January insurrection. Matthew Valasik and Shannon Reid, authors of *Alt-Right Gangs: A Hazy Shade of White*, explain to *Salon* that 'some members have left extremist groups in the wake of the Jan. 6 violence. The members who remain, and the new members they are attracting, are increasing the radicalisation of far-right groups. As the less committed members abandon these far-right groups, only the more devout remain.'[1]

This shift, they say, could alter the subculture of those groups, driving them increasingly further right. In turn, this could accelerate reactionary behaviour and extremist tendencies within the groups.

The pandemic also played a role in driving people towards more extremist beliefs. Charities such as Hope Not Hate saw a rise in online radicalisation as early as the 2020 lockdown. Increased time spent isolated, online and unsure of the future in such an uncertain world has driven people into dangerous communities where they seek answers and a sense of safety. As Elle Reeve wrote for CNN: 'Hate groups are taking advantage of this unprecedented moment; an increased amount of time online, compounded by feelings of uncertainty, a lack of meaningful social engagement and decreased supervision has increased young people's susceptibility to radicalisation.'[2]

Julia Ebner, author of *Going Dark* and its follow-up, *Going Mainstream*, argues that the far right and radical right have also been very successful in mainstreaming their politics, shifting the Overton window in their favour and making beliefs and ideologies that only a decade ago would have been considered extreme acceptable in mainstream political discourse. In an interview over Zoom, she tells me that 'I think one of the biggest wins has been that they've really managed to leak some of their language, their key concepts and narratives and even their symbols and their memes into mainstream public discourse, and even political discourse'. In this way, the ideologies that originate in far-right communities move through the pipeline, as explained by Sian Norris in Chapter 5.

But it's important to acknowledge that this is not just a bottom-up process. Far-right politics and beliefs have always existed within electoral and party politics, and this is also fed down to the electorate. To say that racist, male supremacist, cis-heteropatriarchal ideas only infiltrate politics because of extremists online glosses over the vast history of power, oppression and colonialism that has always been at the heart of the political realm. As Sam Moore and Alex Roberts explain in *Post-Internet Far Right*, the state and the far right are symbiotic: 'the state requires the far-right to support electorally its expansion of control over heavily policed communities, and the far right needs the state as a foil for its anger and campaigns'.[3]

The far right never demands anything radical, or liberating, or that goes against state interest, such as abolition of the police and carceral system, freedom of movement or an end to colonial domination or gender-based exploitation. These are the kinds of demands that communists or anarchists might make. Instead, despite often considering themselves anti-government, the far right's main complaint is that the state is not going far enough with its promises of power: promises of policing and control, of closed borders, of deportation and other forms of necropolitics, of entrenching the supremacy of men and the heterosexual family through state-based education. 'Rishi should have stuck with Suella and followed through with promises he made to the British public to stop the boats', Tommy Robinson posted in his Telegram channel following the resignation of Minister for Immigration Robert Jenrick, a quintessential example of the types of pronouncements he posts daily.

If far-right and populist politics aren't going away, how do we stop people, including women, from being drawn into radical movements? Unfortunately, there isn't a simple answer. But one idea that was echoed by almost all the experts I spoke to for this book (and the preceding podcast) was that the right and far right are using a plurality of tactics, from online propaganda to lobbying mainstream politics, street violence and disinformation and misinformation campaigns, to name just a few. It follows that we cannot fight back in just one way. There are numerous ways to resist, and we must use as many as possible. We now discuss some of the ways already being implemented, by charities, research bodies, feminist groups and activists.

Education

It is through the lens of the far right as an extension of mainstream politics that the IRMS approaches their work. Alex DiBranco points to the privatisation movement in the US, which grew out of desegregation and the goal to fill education with all white, male academics to, in part, promote abstinence-only education, as an example of where the roots of incel culture and male supremacy are buried. 'So we really advocate for comprehensive, consent-based sex education as an important intervention point', she explains.

She goes on to say that in IRMS training sessions, concerned parents often ask what to do if their school board is taken over by QAnon or Proud Boys supporters, a tactic both movements have adopted in order to push bans targeting books with LGBTQ+ and critical race theory themes. 'We say to them, don't wait! If you have a social justice-oriented school board to begin with, it's much harder for them to make inroads than if we're reactive.' Much of the intervention focused on incel and misogynistic extremism that she sees tends to use appeals which actually *align* with male supremacist ideals. 'They'll use the protection of women and that kind of language to talk about what it means to be a man. So you end up with men who are maybe not participating in violence, that are still some version of conservative, racist, misogynist, sexist, being given speaking engagements to speak about being formers.' Instead, she believes that this is another area where early intervention can be more useful.

Other charities, notably Hope Not Hate in the UK, have stressed the importance of educating teachers themselves on how to spot the signs of far-right radicalisation or grooming. Discussing a 57-page guidebook the charity launched for schools in 2021, Owen Jones, the Director of Education and Training, tells the *Guardian* that he believes heightened anxiety caused by the pandemic has left children more vulnerable to being drawn into far-right pipelines. 'They are also having fewer social interactions with people who could take them off the wrong path', he says, adding that 'teachers may not be aware of the telltale signs, such as a students using language picked up in incel communities'.[4] The popularity of Andrew Tate has highlighted the importance for teachers to be educated about and able to facilitate discussions around male supremacy, anti-feminism and other far-right gateways. A 2023 YouGov poll found that 54 per cent of children between 6 and 15 had heard of Tate, with that number increasing to 60 per cent in boys, one in six of whom said they had a 'positive opinion' of the former kick-boxer.[5]

Some schools have already implemented lesson plans and classes where children can discuss Tate and challenge the statements he makes about women (and minorities). As well as discussing the content that influencers such as Tate produce, online disinformation experts also suggest that educating young people on how algorithms work – that they don't necessarily promote the most popular content but rather that which will drive the most engagement by causing an emotional response – can help them better understand what they're seeing online and why.

Tech moderation and regulation

Tech companies also need to play a role. As Eviane Leidig observes in her book *The Women of the Far Right*, there are three main ways tech and social media giants such as X, Facebook and YouTube can tackle the spread of far-right propaganda: deplatforming, demonetising and demotion.[6] Deplatforming involves banning specific people or communities from a platform. Since 2016, many of the most famous faces of the far right have been deplatformed from various sites, including Trump, who was famously booted off X in the wake of 6 January (X chairman Elon Musk reinstated his account in November 2022). Laura Loomer, Milo Yiannopoulos, Paul Joseph Watson and other contributors to the conspiracy website Infowars have also been shown the door from platforms such as Facebook.

While contentious, there is some evidence to suggest that banning far-right influencers does limit the reach of their ideas. 'Extremists can reach more people on these popular platforms; in addition to recruiting new members, they can influence mainstream discussions and narratives in a way they can't on more niche alternative platforms', writes social media journalist Shirin Ghaffary. However, she explains that while some of the studies into deplatforming far-right radicals 'have found that deplatforming was effective as a short-term solution in reducing the reach and influence of offensive accounts ... some studies found increases in toxic behaviour these users exhibited on alternative platforms'.[7]

Demonetising is the act of removing a creator's ability to earn revenue from their content via views. Although limiting a creator's income can impact their ability to create, organise and sustain themselves, it doesn't stop their *ideas* from spreading online. There may be less incentive to post, but what they do post is still reaching its audience. However, some activists and experts continue to work together to undermine far-right content creators' ability to make money from generating hate. '[T]hese influencers find whatever's hot in the news, whatever's garnering a lot of attention, and they manipulate it to their agenda so they can monetize the results to their followers', Heidi Beirich, co-founder of the Global Project Against Hate and Extremism, explained to the *Washington Post*. In the same article, Nandini Jammi, one of the co-founders of Sleeping Giants – an organisation that pressures advertisers to block their ads from appearing on far-right content creators' channels, thereby choking their monetary supply – explained how she worked with platforms including SoundCloud and Mailchimp to demonetise right-wing commentators Andy Ngo and Stefan Molyneux. 'These bad actors have made a business out of publishing increasingly extreme and hateful content because it makes them money. With that money, they're able to expand their operations. They can hire new influencers and writers to scale the production of content around these narratives that they've built', she told the *Post*.[8] Within six months of launching Sleeping Giants, Jammi had reportedly cost Breitbart 90 per cent of its advertising revenue.[9] Finally there is demotion, colloquially known as 'shadow banning', in which content containing specific words or phrases or originating from specific accounts is not picked up by recommendation algorithms, meaning it does not reach as wide an audience. Shadow banning is often held up by far-right actors as proof that they are *saying things the establishment is afraid of*, which furthers their victim/silent majority narratives and acts as a cover for lack of engagement or reach. There's still some debate about whether shadow banning actually exists or how effective it is if it does.[10]

In an article for *Internet Policy Review*, researchers from Swansea University and the University of Amsterdam propose a 'co-regulatory' approach to this kind of social media moderation, one in which tech companies, states and civil society 'can fully participate … to find the solution to the issue of the amplification of borderline and extremist content'. This, they argue, would be more beneficial than single regulatory approaches, as it would avoid the 'accountability gap' that results from social media companies creating self-regulatory bodies, as well as the issue of handing policy-making over to programmers.[11]

The researchers also suggest that this type of co-regulation would help to tackle the challenge of what they call 'borderline content', which does not specifically break any laws or platform regulations but may still cause harm or lead to radicalisation.[12] As we've seen throughout this book, far-right content creators have become skilled at dodging content moderation systems in a number of ways, including adopting algospeak and complex sociolects (the dialect used by particular social group), among other tactics.

Women may also be less likely to be affected by content moderation because, as we've seen, they typically fit the demographic promoted by recommendation algorithms and create content that is less overtly political, focusing instead on the lifestyle aspect of far-right movements.

While social media companies certainly have a part to play in containing the spread of digital far-right propaganda, I remain sceptical of their ability to do so given their function, structure and goals. Social media companies, despite having become a form of infrastructure that is indispensable in many of our lives, ultimately exist to make money; specifically, to make a small group of people very rich. Divisive, polarising and increasingly extreme content, particularly that provokes anger and outrage, keeps people engaged – and engagement is what drives revenue. As various scholars have pointed out, particularly Afrofuturist and Black cyber scholars researching technology, many of the mechanisms that have allowed, even encouraged, extremism to thrive online are built into the ideological foundations of Silicon Valley.

Some of the most notable financiers and forefathers of Silicon Valley follow an accelerationist school of thought. Others, including Peter Thiel and the Koch Brothers, are disaster capitalists, profiteering from inequality and the looming climate collapse. How can we expect social media and tech companies to address radicalisation if it isn't a side effect of these technologies but a function? As Jessie Daniels writes:

The view that circulates in popular understandings of the alt-right and of tech culture by mostly White liberal writers, scholars, and journalists is one in which racism is a 'bug' rather than a 'feature' of the system. They report with alarm that there's racism on the Internet (or, in the last election), as if this is a revelation, or they 'journey' into the heart of the racist right, as if it isn't everywhere in plain sight.[13]

In the 18 months I have spent monitoring far-right digi-spheres for this book, I have not 'journeyed' anywhere. I did it all from the comfort of my sofa, using several fake accounts, an old phone, a SIM card I bought in cash and a sturdy VPN to protect my safety as a queer person. I downloaded Telegram and started searching for all the dog whistles and far-right keywords I could think of. Within minutes, I had joined about ten channels. My housemate, watching over my shoulder, as much as I tried to discourage her, suggested simply searching for the word 'fascist'. 'They're not going to have channels called "the fascist channel where we do fascism!"', I retorted, but we tried it anyway and four or so channels popped up (all of which I, as Ava, joined).

Following far-right creators was just as simple. I searched on Instagram, YouTube, Twitter and Facebook for the names familiar to me from my previous research and went through their following lists to find more accounts. As we discussed in previous chapters, these creators repost each other frequently, so my following count quickly grew. Soon, all the platforms were suggesting other far-right accounts for Ava to follow, all based on who the followers of accounts I already followed were interacting with.

Only once on Telegram was I asked to verify my identity to join a channel, and that was an automated prompt asking me to solve a maths problem. On Facebook, about half of the private groups I asked to join (the majority of which were gender critical groups) had a questionnaire to fill out, mostly asking for the reason why you wanted to join the group or to see if your beliefs were aligned with theirs. Only once was my completely blank Facebook profile rejected. There is no gatekeeping or security you need to overcome to access websites such as Stormfront. You simply type in the URL like you would for ASOS or the BBC. While several Reddit communities, including the largest incel subreddit, have been quarantined, they still pop up immediately if you directly type in the URL rather than searching for them onsite. Finding the link for the r/incels only took a few minutes of Googling and, ironically, I accessed it via a direct link from a news article written about the group from before its quarantine. While I would have had to do a call to join the organising channel of more politically focused groups such as PA, several others had omni-directional organising livechats easily accessible via Facebook groups. I did not need to use the Tor browser or have any kind of tech skills. In fact, throughout my research, several friends sent me posts with far-right themes that had come up in their recommended content channels, having never interacted with that kind of content before.

I think I've driven my point home enough. We need to move past the misconception of far-right communities as 'dark, murky' parts of the internet. They are a feature of its landscape; one that is not only easy to walk into but often barges into our path even if we try to avoid it.

Further, as technology develops, how will we stay one step ahead of the ways the far right will manipulate it for propaganda? This has always been a strength of the far right, from Hitler's use of the wireless to neo-Nazis using DBS to dodge hate speech censorship. And, as we saw in Chapter 5, the far right is already jumping on AI to spread disinformation and misinformation using machine-generated images and videos. As this technology improves and becomes harder to distinguish from 'real' content, how will we mitigate it? This is why teaching digital literacy is so key to combating radicalisation, Julia Ebner tells me. Instead of just looking at how to distinguish disinformation and misinformation and propaganda, we need to teach people about the psychology behind it:

> We often talk about 'how can we distinguish disinformation or fake news from reliable sources?' But what's a lot more troubling is how do we behave? Or how can we cope in new social media environments? And in new online group dynamics? How can we make sure that a hobby community that we joined doesn't all of a sudden drive us into a very extreme direction, which happens so often in gaming or in a specific music scene,

or in a specific kind of fitness community or yoga community, which might start as something very unpolitical and something very innocent but then is leveraged by extremists and becomes more political and more also more radicalised?

The way we teach and talk about digital literacy, and perhaps even the way social media companies approach moderation, needs to be more holistic than reactive. Rather than playing cat and mouse with new technologies, memes, dog whistles and movements, we should instead focus our energy on building resistance to hate taking root in our lives. Because we all have weak spots in our worldviews that could be exploited, cracked open by the right argument and leave us vulnerable to radicalisation. Here again, we can also see the role of education as an early intervention tactic.

Building resilient communities

We also need to ask ourselves some tough questions about how we got here and what sort of society we want to build in place of one where far-right politics and extremism can thrive. 'We need to address sexism in our society at multiple levels', says Emily Gorcenski, noting that one way of doing this is by better preparing educators and parents to recognise signs of radicalisation in young people and intervene. To this end, she says we need to reframe how we address racial, sexual and other identity-based inequality, moving away from an anti-discrimination lens:

We have to acknowledge that people are not on equal footing now, even though they should be. In order to correct those wrongs, we do need to look at the power dynamics. And if we are unable to honestly and consistently acknowledge that there are power dynamic differences, all of the anti-discrimination in the world is only going to reinforce those power differences.

Many feminist groups are already working to address this, particularly intersectional feminist groups such as Sisters Uncut, a London-based collective that opposes cuts to services for survivors of sexualised and intimate partner violence. 'Sisters Uncut articulates a politics based on grappling with these questions, undoing both gender and race by rejecting the law enforcement that protects the property of whiteness', writes Alison Phipps in an essay on Sisters Uncut's Kill the Bill campaign,[14] which arose alongside their actions against the Metropolitan Police Service following the murder of Sarah Everard by off-duty officer Wayne Couzens in 2021. In this essay, and in her book *Me Not You*, Phipps argues that it is only through intersectional action – which recognises that women can be oppressed on the basis of gender while also benefiting from oppression on the basis of race, class, naturalised status or even gender identity or sexuality – that we can begin to move forwards as a collective. As Gorcenski puts it: 'To prevent women from being radicalised, we have to address the fact that women and girls are treated differently and they're starting from a different basis. And so we have to acknowledge that in order to achieve the goals of equality, we have to address the wrongs of the past.'

Feminist Fightback, an anti-capitalist feminist collective, provides another example of how feminist groups can directly address the issue of women's radicalisation. The group runs workshops dedicated to exploring the gender politics of the far right. These consist of panel talks hosted by other groups and activists, including the Trans Safety Network and London Anti-Fascist Assembly, as well as interactive sessions in which participants map far-right attacks on abortion, trans rights and sex education, as well as suggesting ideas for resistance. Here, we can see how feminist movements seek to understand the ways in which gender is a key factor in the rise of far-right politics and to explore ways to create communities that are resistant to far-right radicalisation.

As several experts have pointed out to me, mitigating against radicalisation or even deradicalising people should not involve validating the 'concerns' that lead them towards radical communities. Instead, it should seek to ground them back in reality. The unfortunate truth is that reality is complicated, and uncomfortable, and contradictory, and unfair. One of the most enticing things the far right offers is simple answers to some of the world's biggest issues. Our world is only getting more complicated and it will continue to do so as the effects of the climate disaster become more pronounced, first on majority world countries, which will create a wave of climate refugees, and then on minority world countries where populist leaders will promise ever more convenient, necro-political and authoritarian policies to a scared and hungry populace.

But it doesn't have to be this way. We can build strong communities with infrastructures of support, solidarity and mutual aid. We can withdraw consent from policing, strong men with simple answers and tech companies monetising our despair. Hope can be revolutionary, but without putting it into action, it amounts to little more than daydreaming. In our day-to-day lives, we can find ways to resist the rising tide of the far right. Several of the experts I spoke to emphasised the importance of education and having difficult, open conversations with the people in our lives about politics and oppression.

In order to address the issue of women in the far right, or why women keep joining the far right, we have to be much better at something we are taught not to do: we have to see women as actual people. People who are capable of harm. People who can be harmed. People who can be both survivors and aggressors. People who are capable of hate. People who are capable of change. People who are lost causes. Because the tide of the far right is rising across the globe, particularly in the imperial core, and it isn't just coming in the form of strongman politicians, Brown Shirts marching through the streets or even boys with semi-automatic weapons and manifestos posted online. It's women with fairy-light backdrops extolling the virtues of traditional womanhood. It's mums in Telegram chats and forums talking about isolating their trans child and organising fundraisers for their husbands to attend the Capitol riot. It's women in their twenties chartering boats to intercept migrant rescues in the Mediterranean. It's teenage girls – your daughter, sister or cousin – bullying each other on Tumblr to the point of self-harm for not being racist enough. It's hot, single women in your area and they're looking to meet you.

Acknowledgements

Writing a book can feel like an extremely solitary process while you're in it: you spend hundreds of hours alone, chipping away at a project that usually has just your name on the cover. But, upon reflection, you always realise just how much of a communal effort it was, and if you're being honest with yourself, others deserve to have their name splashed on it too.

I'd like to start by thanking Jon Curzon, my agent, without whom this project would not have found a home. Thank you for believing that this book could be a reality and that the idea I presented to you deserved to see the light of day. Thank you also for being an ongoing source of support and encouragement throughout the process. I hope this is the start of a long professional relationship.

Second, I'd like to thank Alun Richards for his patient and diligent editing, which wrangled this project into something legible and worth reading, and Kim Walker for stewarding me through the process with Manchester University Press. Further, I'd like to thank Dan Harding for his eagle-eyed copyediting.

I'd also like to acknowledge the several experts and interviewees who enthusiastically shared their knowledge and insight with me, not only for this project but the podcast that preceded it. In particular, I'd like to thank Dr Eviane Leidig, whose research has not only been an inspiration for me but who continues to be a source of insight, encouragement and support as I report on the far right.

Furthermore, I'd like to voice my appreciation for Hackney's libraries, which offered me a sheltered, comfortable, welcoming place where I could access free Wi-Fi and enjoy the company of my neighbours while working on this book. I hope to spend many more hours writing in them in the future.

This book happened to coincide with a very difficult time in my life, and without the love and support of my friends, I not only would not have finished this project but probably would have fallen apart entirely. While this was a joint effort and one all my friends were deeply involved with, for this book I particularly have to thank Alex and Eddie. Thank you Alex, who supported this book by regularly cooking me dinner, yelling at me to rest, listening patiently to my theories and basically organising the entire house-moving process while I was distracted. I love you so, so much. Eddie, thank you for saving me literally hundreds of pounds by downloading countless academic articles for me, sending me source suggestions, explaining AI to me and for generally being a wonderful friend.

Acknowledgements

I'd also like to thank Dr Toby Atkinson, who was added to a group chat with me by a mutual friend two years ago because 'you both like talking about gender and the far right' and in that time has suggested dozens of sources to me and helped me tease out new ideas and threads of investigation. I owe you a pint.

Finally, thanks goes to my mum and sister, two of the strongest women I know: I'm so lucky I had you both through this and I'm so proud of us for getting to the other side. This book is for you both, too.

Further reading

Banet-Weiser, Sarah, and Kate M. Miltner. '#MasculinitySo-Fragile: Culture, Structure, and Networked Misogyny'. Feminist Media Studies, vol. 16, no. 1, 22 December 2015, pp. 171–174, https://doi.org/10.1080/14680777.2016.11204 90. Accessed 12 April 2019.

Darby, Seyward. Sisters in Hate: American Women on the Front Lines of White Nationalism. Little Brown And Company, 2020.

Evie Magazine. 'About Us'. www.eviemagazine.com/about. Accessed 4 July 2024.

Futrelle, David. 'We Hunted the Mammoth Is Coming Soon'. We Hunted the Mammoth, www.wehuntedthemammoth. com/2018/08/01/has-been-pickup-artist-roosh-v-sounds-more-like-an-incel-every-day/. Accessed 6 December 2023.

Geller, Lisa B., et al. 'The Role of Domestic Violence in Fatal Mass Shootings in the United States, 2014–2019'. Injury Epidemiology, vol. 8, no. 1, 31 May 2021, injepijournal. biomedcentral.com/articles/10.1186/s40621-021-00330-0, https://doi.org/10.1186/s40621-021-00330-0. Accessed 16 March 2024.

GirlDefined. 'Meet Us'. girldefined.com/meet-us. Accessed 4 July 2024.

Institute for Research on Male Supremacism. 'What Is Male Supremacism?' www.theirms.org/what-is-male-supremacism. Accessed 16 March 2024.

ISD. 'Groypers'. www.isdglobal.org/explainers/groypers/. Accessed 16 April 2023.

Further reading

Iyer, Prithvi, and Shruti Jain. 'An Unlikely Match: Women and the Far-Right'. Orfonline.org, 4 January 2021, www.orfonline. org/expert-speak/unlikely-match-women-far-right. Accessed 17 March 2024.

Jennings, Rebecca. 'Are We All Influencers Now?' Vox, 1 March 2023, www.vox.com/the-goods/23618956/influencer-indus try-emily-hund. Accessed 29 February 2024.

Lorenz, Taylor. 'Meet the Woman behind Libs of TikTok, Secretly Fueling the Right's Outrage Machine'. Washington Post, 19 April 2022, www.washingtonpost.com/technology/20 22/04/19/libs-of-tiktok-right-wing-media/. Accessed 16 March 2024.

Maiberg, Emanuel. 'Why the Guardian Censored Judith Butler on TERFs'. Vice, 8 September 2021, www.vice.com/en/ article/7kv3m4/why-the-guardian-censored-judith-butler-on-terfs. Accessed 16 May 2023.

Mulhall, Joe. Drums in the Distance. Icon Books, 2021.

Nelson, Alondra. Afrofuturism. Duke University Press, 2002.

Nelson, Alondra, Thuy Linh Nguyen Tu and Alicia Headlam Hines (eds). Technicolor: Race, Technology, and Everyday Life. NYU Press, 2001.

Noble, Safiya. Algorithms of Oppression: How Search Engines Reinforce Racism. New York University Press, 2018.

Phipps, Alison. 'White Feminism and the Racial Capitalist Protection Racket: From #MeToo to Me, Not You'. Phipps. space, 7 May 2021, phipps.space/2021/05/07/protection-racket/. Accessed 20 August 2023.

Russell, Legacy. Glitch Feminism: A Manifesto. Verso, 2020.

Shah, Areeba. 'Libs of TikTok Owner Chaya Raichik Ramps up Her Anti-LGBTQ Crusade'. Salon, 24 January 2023, www.salon.com/2023/01/24/libsof-tiktok-owner-chaya-raichik-ramps-up-her-anti-lgbtq-crusade/. Accessed 29 February 2024.

Stewart, Alya. 'About Us'. Wifewithapurpose.com, wifewith apurpose.com/About-us/. Accessed 16 April 2023.

Wilkie, Aaron R., and James E. B. Brough. 'Men Resist Green Behavior as Unmanly'. Scientific American, 26 December 2017, www.scientificamerican.com/article/men-resist-gree n-behavior-as-unmanly/. Accessed 23 August 2023.

Notes

INTRODUCTION

1 Dworkin, Andrea. Right-Wing Women: The Politics of Domesticated Females. The Women's Press, 1988, p. 13.
2 Change Research. 'Young Women Are More Liberal than Young Men'. Change Research, 18 September 2023, https://changeresearch.com/young-women-are-more-liberal-than-young-men/. Accessed 8 February 2024.
3 Pew Research Center. 'Public Opinion on Abortion'. https://www.pewresearch.org/religion/fact-sheet/public-opinion-on-abortion/. Accessed 13 May 2024.
4 Pew Research Center. 'The Global Divide on Homosexuality'. Pew Research Center's Global Attitudes Project, 4 June 2013, www.pewresearch.org/global/2013/06/04/the-global-divide-on-homosexuality/. Accessed 8 February 2024.
5 Smith, Matthew. 'Where Does the British Public Stand on Transgender Rights in 2022?' Yougov.co.uk, 20 July 2022, yougov.co.uk/society/articles/43194-where-does-british-public-stand-transgender-rights-1. Accessed 8 February 2024.
6 Zainulbhai, Hani. 'Women, More than Men, Say Climate Change Will Harm Them Personally'. Pew Research Center, 2 December 2015, www.pewresearch.org/short-reads/2015/12/02/women-more-than-men-say-climate-change-will-harm-them-personally/. Accessed 8 February 2024.
7 Inglehart, Ronald, and Pippa Norris. 'The Developmental Theory of the Gender Gap: Women's and Men's Voting Behavior in Global Perspective'. International Political Science Review, vol. 21, no. 4, October 2000, pp. 441–463,

journals.sagepub.com/doi/pdf/10.1177/0192512100214007, https://doi.org/10.1177/0192512100214007. Accessed 16 March 2024.

8 Daniels, Jessie. Nice White Ladies: The Truth about White Supremacy, Our Role in It, and How We Can Help Dismantle It. Seal Press, 2021.

9 Do Couto, Sarah. 'Femcels: Inside the Enigmatic Subculture of Involuntary Celibate Women'. Global News, 2 February 2023, globalnews.ca/news/9449316/femcel-definition-soci al-media-sex-gender-incels/. Accessed 3 July 2024.

10 Daniels, Nice White Ladies.

11 Do Couto, 'Femcels'.

12 Amery, Fran, and Aurelien Mondon. 'Othering, Peaking, Populism and Moral Panics: The Reactionary Strategies of Organised Transphobia'. Sociological Review, 16 April 2024, https://doi.org/10.1177/00380261241242283. Accessed 3 July 2024.

13 Leidig, Eviane. The Women of the Far Right. Columbia University Press, 2023.

14 Hope Not Hate. 'The International Alternative Right: An Explainer'. https://hopenothate.org.uk/wp-content/upload s/2019/07/Alt-Right-report-SHORT-2019-v1.pdf. Accessed 8 February 2024.

15 European Center for Populism Studies. 'Far or Extreme Right'. www.populismstudies.org/Vocabulary/far-or-extreme-right/. Accessed 3 July 2024.

16 Mason, Paul. How to Stop Fascism. Penguin, 2021, p. xxi.

1 GIRL-FASCISM DEFINED: UNDERSTANDING THE ALT-RIGHT AND FAR RIGHT

1 Allchorn, Dr William. 'Turning back to Biologised Racism: A Content Analysis of Patriotic Alternative UK's Online Discourse'. GNET, 22 February 2021, https://gnet-resear ch.org/2021/02/22/turning-back-to-biologised-racism-a-con tent-analysis-of-patriotic-alternative-uks-online-discourse/. Accessed 12 February 2024.

2 Hope Not Hate. 'What Is the Manosphere? The People vs the 'Elite'? State of Hate 2019'. Hopenothate.org.uk, 18

February 2019, hopenothate.org.uk/2019/02/18/state-of-hate-2019-manosphere-explained/. Accessed 4 December 2023.

3 Lovett, Ian, and Adam Nagourney. 'Video Rant, then Deadly Rampage in California Town'. New York Times, 24 May 2014, www.nytimes.com/2014/05/25/us/california-drive-by-shooting.html. Accessed 12 February 2024.

4 Bates, Laura. Men Who Hate Women: From Incels to Pickup Artists – The Truth about Extreme Misogyny and How It Affects Us All. Sourcebooks, 2020, p. 42.

5 Davies, Shaun, and Milly Stilinovich. 'How Return of Kings Used Outrage to Sell Extreme Ideas'. BBC News, 4 February 2016, www.bbc.co.uk/news/world-australia-35490223. Accessed 4 December 2023.

6 West, Lindy. 'Now Roosh v and His Band of Sad Men in Dark Rooms Know How It Feels to Be Bombarded with Bile'. The Guardian, 7 February 2016, www.theguardian.com/commentisfree/2016/feb/07/daryush-roosh-v-valizadeh-and-his-acolytes-pilloried. Accessed 4 December 2023.

7 Chadwick Galt, B. 'How to Overthrow the New Master Race: Western Women'. Manosphere.at, 13 June 2018, manosphere.at/2018/06/13/how-to-overthrow-the-new-master-race-western-women/. Accessed 13 August 2024.

8 Pew Research Center. 'An Examination of the 2016 Electorate, Based on Validated Voters'. Pew Research Center, U.S. Politics & Policy, 9 August 2018, www.pewresearch.org/politics/2018/08/09/an-examination-of-the-2016-electorate-based-on-validated-voters/. Accessed 3 July 2024.

9 Ball, Molly. 'Donald Trump Didn't Really Win 52% of White Women in 2016'. Time, 18 October 2018, https://time.com/5422644/trump-white-women-2016/. Accessed 4 December 2023.

10 Pew Research Center. 'An Examination of the 2016 Electorate, Based on Validated Voters'.

11 Donegan, Moira. 'Half of White Women Continue to Vote Republican: What's Wrong with Them?' The Guardian, 9 November 2018, www.theguardian.com/commentisfree/2018/nov/09/white-women-vote-republican-why. Accessed 3 July 2024.

12 Eisenstein, Zillah. 'Hillary Clinton's Imperial Feminism'. The Cairo Review of Global Affairs, 23 October 2016, www. thecairoreview.com/essays/hillary-clintons-imperial-femi nism/. Accessed 3 July 2024.

13 Southern Poverty Law Center. 'Alt-Right'. Southern Poverty Law Center, 2014, www.splcenter.org/fighting-hate/extrem ist-files/ideology/alt-right. Accessed 4 December 2023.

14 ADL. 'Steve Bannon: Five Things to Know'. Adl.org, 2018, www.adl.org/resources/backgrounder/steve-bannon-five-th ings-know. Accessed 3 July 2024.

15 Cameron, Chris. 'These Are the People Who Died in Connection with the Capitol Riot'. New York Times, 5 January 2022, www.nytimes.com/2022/01/05/us/politics/ jan-6-capitol-deaths.html. Accessed 3 July 2024.

16 Thompson, Jack, and George Hawley. 'Does the Alt-Right Still Matter? An Examination of Alt-Right Influence between 2016 and 2018'. Nations and Nationalism, vol. 27, no. 4, 8 July 2021, https://doi.org/10.1111/nana.12736. Accessed 29 February 2024.

17 ADL. 'Alt Right: A Primer on the New White Supremacy'. Adl.org, 10 February 2016, www.adl.org/resources/back grounder/alt-right-primer-new-white-supremacy. Accessed 4 December 2023.

18 Darby, Seyward. Sisters in Hate: American Woman and White Extremism. Back Bay Books, 2021, p. 11.

19 Donovan, Joan, et al. Meme Wars. Bloomsbury, 2022; Daniels, Jessie. 'The Algorithmic Rise of the "Alt-Right"'. Contexts, vol. 17, no. 1, February 2018, pp. 60–65, https:// doi.org/10.1177/1536504218766547. Accessed 3 July 2024.

20 Hawley, George. 'The Demography of the Alt-Right'. Institute for Family Studies, 2018, ifstudies.org/blog/the-demography-of-the-alt-right. Accessed 3 July 2024.

21 Matfess, Hilary, and Devorah Margolin. The Women of January 6th: A Gendered Analysis of the 21st Century American Far-Right. Program on Extremism, 2022.

22 Dickson, E. J. 'How Do Women Become White Supremacists?' Rolling Stone, 15 July 2020, www.rollingstone.com/culture/ culture-features/seyward-darby-sisters-in-hate-female-whi te-supremacists-1029109/. Accessed 4 December 2023.

Notes

2 FORWARD TO THE PAST: THE HISTORY OF WOMEN IN FAR-RIGHT MOVEMENTS

1 Mosse, G. L. 'The Mystical Origins of National Socialism'. Journal of the History of Ideas, vol. 22, no. 1, January 1961, p. 81, https://doi.org/10.2307/2707875. Accessed 5 November 2023.

2 Liyanage, Chamila. 'Savitri Devi and the Radical Right's Fascination with Esoteric Nazism'. Rantt.com, 17 July 2020, https://rantt.com/savitri-devi-and-the-radical-rights-fascination-with-esoteric-nazism. Accessed 8 October 2024.

3 Ross, Alexander Reid. Against the Fascist Creep. AK Press, 2017, p. 52.

4 Gordon, Linda. 'How Women in the KKK Were Instrumental to Its Rise'. BuzzFeed News, 17 August 2017, www.buzzfeednews.com/article/lindagordon/how-women-in-the-kkk-were-instrumental-to-its-rise. Accessed 4 December 2023.

5 Smith, Laura. 'No, Talking about Women's Role in White Supremacy Is Not Blaming Women'. Medium, 21 February 2018, http://timeline.com/no-talking-about-womens-role-in-white-supremacy-is-not-blaming-women-f16739c46665. Accessed 6 December 2022.

6 Smith, Laura. 'One Woman's Effort to Mix Klan-Style Hatred with Wholesome Christian Values'. Medium, 10 January 2018, http://timeline.com/one-womans-effort-to-mix-klan-style-hatred-with-wholesome-christian-values-d02db50620e8. Accessed 6 December 2022.

7 Smith, 'One Woman's Effort to Mix Klan-Style Hatred with Wholesome Christian Values'.

8 Henriquez, Natalie. '"The Malicious and Untruthful White Press: Ida B Wells's Fight against White Supremacy in the Contemporary Age', Historical Perspectives: Santa Clara University Undergraduate Journal of History, Series II, vol. 26, no. 10, 2021, https://scholarcommons.scu.edu/historical-perspectives/vol26/iss1/10. Accessed 3 July 2024.

9 Passmore, Kevin. Fascism: A Very Short Introduction. Oxford University Press, 2014.

10 Pugh, Martin. 'These British Women Fought and Won the Vote. Then They Joined the Fascist Movement'. Slate

Notes

Magazine, 14 April 2017, http://slate.com/news-and-polit ics/2017/04/why-the-british-union-fascist-movement-appe aled-to-so-many-women.html. Accessed 3 July 2024.

11 Pugh, 'These British Women Fought and Won the Vote'.

12 Parsons, Vic. '"Gender-Critical" Feminism Is Just Trans-phobic'. Vice.com, 27 April 2023, https://web.archive.org/ web/20230427112459/www.vice.com/en/feature/4a3vji/ge nder-critical-feminism-isnt-feminist-its-just-transphobic. Accessed 4 July 2024.

13 Phipps, Alison. Me, Not You: The Trouble with Mainstream Feminism. Manchester University Press, 2020.

14 Beck, Koa. White Feminism. Simon & Schuster Ltd, 2021, p. 26.

15 Trippenbach, Ivanne, and Franck Johannès. 'Le Pen Loses French Election but Launches "the Great Battle for the Legislative Elections"'. Le Monde, 25 April 2022, www.lem onde.fr/en/2022-presidential-election/article/2022/04/25/ marine-le-pen-loses-french-presidential-election-but-carri es-on-with-her-political-commitment_5981535_16.html. Ac-cessed 4 July 2024.

16 BBC Newsround. 'French President Emmanuel Macron Calls Snap Election'. BBC, 10 June 2024, www.bbc.co.uk/ newsround/articles/cqll4072g5wo. Accessed 13 August 2024.

17 AP News. 'France Election Highlights: Leftists Win Most Seats, but No Party Wins Majority'. AP News, 2024, http:// apnews.com/live/france-election-results-updates-round-2-macron-le-pen#00000190-8f14-ddf4-a7f3-bf3cafb10000. Acc-essed 13 August 2024.

18 Politico. 'France'. Politico, 10 January 2020, www.politico. eu/europe-poll-of-polls/france/. Accessed 13 August 2024.

19 Hope Not Hate. 'Britain First'. Hopenothate.org.uk, 2017, https://hopenothate.org.uk/wp-content/uploads/2017/11/Br itain-First-Army-of-the-Right.pdf. Accessed 4 July 2024.

20 Provost, Claire, and Lara Whyte. 'Why Are Women Joining Far-Right Movements, and Why Are We so Surprised?' OpenDemocracy, 18 January 2019, www.opendemocracy. net/en/5050/women-far-right-movements-why-are-we-sur prised/. Accessed 4 December 2023.

Notes

21 Darby, Seyward. Sisters in Hate: American Women and White Extremism. Back Bay Books, 2021, p. 57.

3 THIS IS WHAT THEY TOOK FROM YOU: THE FAR RIGHT'S VISION FOR WOMEN

1 Institute for Research on Male Supremacism. 'What Is Male Supremacism?' Institute for Research on Male Supremacism, www.theirms.org/what-is-male-supremacism. Accessed 16 March 2024.
2 Norris, Sian. Bodies under Siege. Verso, 2023.
3 Corrêa, Sonia. 'Gender Ideology: Tracking Its Origins and Meanings in Current Gender Politics'. The London School of Economics and Political Science, 11 December 2017, http://blogs.lse.ac.uk/gender/2017/12/11/gender-ideology-tracking-its-origins-and-meanings-in-current-gender-politics/. Accessed 5 December 2023.
4 Oppenheim, Maya. 'Hungarian Prime Minister Viktor Orban Bans Gender Studies Programmes'. The Independent, 24 October 2018, www.independent.co.uk/news/world/europe/hungary-bans-gender-studies-programmes-viktor-or ban-central-european-university-budapest-a8599796.html. Accessed 5 December 2023.
5 Corrêa, Sonia. 'Gender Ideology: Tracking Its Origins and Meanings in Current Gender Politics'. Global Policy Journal, 2018, www.globalpolicyjournal.com/blog/13/02/2018/gen der-ideology-tracking-its-origins-and-meanings-current-gen der-politics. Accessed 13 August 2024.
6 Berkowitz, Bill. '"Cultural Marxism" Catching On'. Southern Poverty Law Center, 15 August 2003, www.splcenter.org/fighting-hate/intelligence-report/2003/cultural-marxi sm-catching. Accessed 22 January 2023.
7 Illing, Sean. 'The Woman at the Center of #Gamergate Gives Zero Fucks about Her Haters'. Vox, 19 September 2017, www.vox.com/culture/2017/9/19/16301682/gamergate-alt-right-zo e-quinn-crash-override-interview. Accessed 4 July 2024.
8 Jason, Zachary. 'Game of Fear'. Boston Magazine, 28 April 2015, www.bostonmagazine.com/news/2015/04/28/gamer gate/. Accessed 4 July 2024.

9 Banet-Weiser, Sarah, and Kate M. Miltner. '#Masculinity-SoFragile: Culture, Structure, and Networked Misogyny'. Feminist Media Studies, vol. 16, no. 1, 22 December 2015, pp. 171–174, https://doi.org/10.1080/14680777.2016.112049 0. Accessed 12 April 2019.

10 'What Is the Manosphere? The People vs the "Elite"? State of Hate 2019'. Hope Not Hate, 18 February 2019, hopenothate.org.uk/2019/02/18/state-of-hate-2019-manosp here-explained/. Accessed 4 December 2023.

11 Beauchamp, Zack. 'A Neo-Nazi Idea to Spark a Race War Inspired the Buffalo Killings'. Vox, 16 May 2022, www.vox. com/policy-and-politics/2022/5/16/23074812/buffalo-shoot ing-accelerationism-great-replacement-neo-nazi. Accessed 4 July 2024.

12 Miller-Idriss, Cynthia. 'White Supremacist Extremism and the Far Right in the U.S.'. Gale.com, 2021, www.gale.com/ intl/essays/cynthia-miller-idriss-white-supremacist-extrem ism-far-right-us. Accessed 21 December 2022.

13 Stanley, Jason. How Fascism Works: The Politics of Us and Them. House, 2018.

14 Khan Academy. 'Women in the 1950s'. Khan Academy, 2008, www.khanacademy.org/humanities/us-history/post warera/1950s-america/a/women-in-the-1950s. Accessed 16 March 2024.

15 Berkowitz, '"Cultural Marxism" Catching On'.

16 Stern, Jessica. 'Going Dark: The Secret Social Lives of Extremists by Julia Ebner Review'. TLS, 26 June 2020, www.the-tls.co.uk/politics-by-region/european-politics/go ing-dark-julia-ebner-review-jessica-stern/. Accessed 4 July 2024.

17 Roosh, Valizadeh. 'Women Must Have Their Behavior and Decisions Controlled by Men'. Rooshv.com, 8 November 2020, http://web.archive.org/web/20201108103001/www.ro oshv.com/women-must-have-their-behavior-and-decisions-controlled-by-men. Accessed 4 July 2024.

18 Kelly, Annie. 'Opinion: The Housewives of White Supremacy'. New York Times, 1 June 2018, www.nytimes.com/20 18/06/01/opinion/sunday/tradwives-women-alt-right.html. Accessed 4 July 2024.

19 Kumaraguru, Yanitra. 'Wages for Housework: A Step towards Equality at First Glance, a Step Away at Second?' King's College London, 19 April 2022, www.kcl.ac.uk/wages-for-housework-a-step-towards-equality-at-first-glance-a-step-aw ay-at-second. Accessed 16 March 2024.

20 Florio, Gina. 'Women Have the Power to End Hookup Culture If They Just Stop Having Casual Sex with Men'. Evie Magazine, 3 April 2023, www.eviemagazine.com/post/ women-have-power-end-hookup-culture-if-just-stop-having-casual-sex-men. Accessed 4 July 2024.

21 Donegan, Moira. 'Sex Positivity Was Fake, but We'll Miss It When It's Gone'. Not the Fun Kind, 7 November 2022, moiradonegan.substack.com/p/sex-positivity-was-fake-but-well. Accessed 4 July 2024.

22 Randall Balmer. 'The Real Origins of the Religious Right'. Politico, 27 May 2014, www.politico.com/magazine/story/ 2014/05/religious-right-real-origins-107133/. Accessed 4 July 2024.

23 Posner, Sarah. 'The Religious Right Is Still Sticking by Trump: Sadly, There's a Long, Grim Pattern'. The Guardian, 5 June 2020, www.theguardian.com/commentisfree/2020/jun/05/ donald-trump-religious-right-george-floyd-racism. Accessed 9 October 2024.

24 Sykes, Sophia. 'Tradwives: The Housewives Commodifying Right-Wing Ideology'. GNET, 7 July 2023, http://gnet-research.org/2023/07/07/tradwives-the-housewives-commo difying-right-wing-ideology/. Accessed 4 July 2024.

25 Sykes, 'Tradwives'.

26 Mattheis, Ashley. 'Shieldmaidens of Whiteness: (Alt) Maternalism and Women Recruiting for the Far/Alt-Right'. Journal for Deradicalization, no. 17, 23 December 2018, pp. 128–162, journals.sfu.ca/jd/index.php/jd/article/ view/177. Accessed 4 July 2024.

27 Pugh, Martin. 'These British Women Fought and Won the Vote. Then They Joined the Fascist Movement'. Slate Magazine, 14 April 2017, http://slate.com/news-and-politics/2017/04/why-the-british-union-fascist-movement-appealed-to-so-many-women.html. Accessed 17 March 2024.

28 Iyer, Prithvi, and Shruti Jain. 'An Unlikely Match: Women and the Far-Right'. Orfonline.org, 4 January 2021, www.orfonline.org/expert-speak/unlikely-match-women-far-right. Accessed 17 March 2024.

29 Burleigh, Nina. 'The Rich Mothers of the Insurrection'. New Republic, 3 February 2021, newrepublic.com/arti cle/161208/trump-women-capitol-riot-funding. Accessed 5 December 2023.

30 Southern Poverty Law Center. 'Moms for Liberty'. Southern Poverty Law Center, nd, www.splcenter.org/fighting-hate/ extremist-files/group/moms-liberty. Accessed 4 July 2024.

31 Friedman, Jonathan, and Nadine Johnson. 'Banned in the USA: The Growing Movement to Censor Books in Schools'. PEN America, 19 September 2022, http://pen.org/report/ banned-usa-growing-movement-to-censor-books-in-schools/. Accessed 5 December 2023.

32 Peterson, Jordan. 'The Gender Scandal: Part One (Scandinavia) and Part Two (Canada)'. Jordanbpeterson.com, 24 February 2019, www.jordanbpeterson.com/political-cor rectness/the-gender-scandal-part-one-scandinavia-and-part-two-canada/. Accessed 4 July 2024.

33 Llanera, Tracy. 'The Misogyny Paradox and the Alt-Right'. Hypatia, 17 March 2023, pp. 1–20, https://doi.org/10.1017/ hyp.2023.4. Accessed 1 April 2023.

34 Jones, Phil. 'Acid Fascism: Past and Present Ties between Occultism and the Far Right'. Verso, 28 June 2021, www.versobooks.com/blogs/5117-acid-fascism-past-and-present-ties-between-occultism-and-the-far-right. Accessed 4 July 2024.

35 Ward, Charlotte, and David Voas. "The Emergence of Conspirituality.' Journal of Contemporary Religion, vol. 26, no. 1, 1 January 2011, pp. 103–121, https://doi.org/10.1080/1 3537903.2011.539846. Accessed 11 March 2021.

36 Ebner, Julia. Going Dark. Bloomsbury, 2021, p. 54.

37 Conroy, J. Oliver. '"Angry White Men": The Sociologist Who Studied Trump's Base before Trump'. The Guardian, 27 February 2017, www.theguardian.com/world/2017/ feb/27/michael-kimmel-masculinity-far-right-angry-white-men. Accessed 4 July 2024.

38 Ebner, Going Dark, p. 54.

39 Farris, Sara R. In the Name of Women's Rights: The Rise of Femonationalism. Duke University Press, 2017.

40 Moore, Sam, and Alex Roberts. Post-Internet Far Right. Dog Section, 2021, p. 125.

41 Dearden, Lizzie. 'Far-Right Protests "Attracting Biggest Numbers since 1930s" in UK amid Brexit Anger, Report Warns'. The Independent, 18 July 2019, www.independent.co.uk/news/uk/home-news/far-right-uk-brexit-muslims-tommy-robinson-protests-extremism-a9011171.html. Accessed 4 July 2024.

42 Dearden, Lizzie. 'Far Right Poses as Protectors of Women to Target Muslims, Official Extremism Report Finds'. The Independent, 7 October 2019, www.independent.co.uk/news/uk/home-news/muslims-extremism-women-far-right-tommy-robinson-rape-a9143671.html. Accessed 4 July 2024.

43 Office for National Statistics. 'Sexual Offences Victim Characteristics, England and Wales'. Ons.gov.uk, 18 March 2021, www.ons.gov.uk/peoplepopulationandcommunity/crimeandjustice/articles/sexualoffencesvictimcharacteristics englandandwales/march2020. Accessed 13 August 2024.

44 Grove, Jennifer, and Jennifer Benner. 'New NISVS Data on Sexual Violence and Sexual Identity: Key Findings and Prevention Recommendations'. National Sexual Violence Resource Center, 10 October 2023, www.nsvrc.org/blogs/new-nisvs-data-sexual-violence-and-sexual-identity-key-findings-and-prevention#:~:text=More%20than%201%20in%204. Accessed 13 August 2024.

45 Penny, Eleanor. 'The Far-Right Talk about Women and Girls the Same Way They Talk about Land and Territory'. New Statesman, 7 December 2018, www.newstatesman.com/politics/2018/12/far-right-talk-about-women-and-girls-same-way-they-talk-about-land-and-territory. Accessed 6 December 2022.

46 Griffin, Susan. Rape: The All-American Crime. Google Books, Copies available through Women Against Rape, 1971, www.google.co.uk/books/edition/Rape/l7PSGwAACAAJ?hl=en. Accessed 4 July 2024.

47 Klaus Theweleit, and Stephen Conway. Male Fantasies: I, Women, Floods, Bodies, History. Translated by Stephen Conway in collaboration with Erica Carter and Chris Turner. Polity Press, 2007.

48 Moore and Roberts, Post-Internet Far Right, p. 35.

49 Berlet, Chip. 'Heroes Know Which Villains to Kill: How Coded Rhetoric Incites Scripted Violence'. Researchgate. net, January 2014, www.researchgate.net/publication/304 590814_Heroes_Know_Which_Villains_to_Kill_How_Cod ed_Rhetoric_Incites_Scripted_Violence. Accessed 13 August 2024.

4 FEMINISM IS CANCER: HOW WOMEN ARE RADICALISED ONLINE

1 Donovan, Joan, et al. Meme Wars. Bloomsbury, 2022, p. 19.

2 CIDOB. 'What Does Radicalisation Look Like? Four Visualisations of Socialisation into Violent Extremism'. CIDOB, 2018, www.cidob.org/es/publicaciones/serie_de_pu blicacion/notes_internacionals/n1_163/what_does_radicali sation_look_like_four_visualisations_of_socialisation_into_ violent_extremism. Accessed 4 July 2024.

3 Von Behr, Ines, et al. 'Radicalisation in the Digital Era: The Use of the Internet in 15 Cases of Terrorism and Extremism'. RAND Corporation, 5 November 2013, www. rand.org/pubs/research_reports/RR453.html. Accessed 4 July 2024.

4 Beam, Louis. 'Leaderless Resistance'. Researchgate.net, 12 February 1992, www.researchgate.net/publication/2330970 25_'Leaderless_resistance'. Accessed 4 July 2024.

5 Abi Wilkinson. 'We Need to Talk about the Online Radicalisation of Young, White Men'. The Guardian, 15 November 2016, www.theguardian.com/commentisfree/ 2016/nov/15/alt-right-manosphere-mainstream-politics-bre itbart. Accessed 4 July 2024.

6 Lewis, Helen. 'How Anti-Feminism Is the Gateway to the Far Right'. The Atlantic, 7 August 2019, www.theatlantic. com/international/archive/2019/08/anti-feminism-gateway- far-right/595642/. Accessed 4 July 2024.

7 Miller-Idriss, Cynthia. 'Opinion: Why the Far-Right Is Really into Home Fitness'. MSNBC.com, 22 March 2022, www.msnbc.com/opinion/msnbc-opinion/pandemic-fitne ss-trends-have-gone-extreme-literally-n1292463. Accessed 4 July 2024.

8 Lewis, Rebecca. Alternative Influence: Broadcasting the Reactionary Right on YouTube. Data and Society, 2018, p. 1.

9 Lewis, Alternative Influence, p. 16.

10 CIDOB. 'What Does Radicalisation Look Like? Four Visualisations of Socialisation into Violent Extremism'. CIDOB, 2018, www.cidob.org/es/publicaciones/serie_de_pu blicacion/notes_internacionals/n1_163/what_does_radicali sation_look_like_four_visualisations_of_socialisation_into_ violent_extremism. Accessed 4 July 2024.

11 Cuda, Amanda. 'We Were Children: I Wasn't the Only Victim'. Connecticut Post, 5 March 2016, www.ctpost.com/ local/article/We-were-children-I-wasn-t-the-only-6872580. php. Accessed 17 March 2024.

12 The Rubin Report. 'On Her Journey from Left to Right: Candace Owens'. YouTube, 28 September 2017, www.you tube.com/watch?v=BSAoitd1BTQ. Accessed 14 December 2019.

13 Nelson, Rebecca. 'Candace Owens Is the New Face of Black Conservatism. But What Does That Really Mean?' Washington Post, 6 March 2019, www.washingtonpost.com/ news/magazine/wp/2019/03/06/feature/candace-owens-is-the-new-face-of-black-conservatism-but-what-does-that-rea lly-mean/. Accessed 4 July 2024.

14 Fruen, Lauren. 'Inside the Trump Winery Wedding of Conservative Activist Candace Owens'. Mail Online, 22 October 2019, www.dailymail.co.uk/news/article-7601719/ PICTURED-Inside-Trump-Winery-wedding-conservative-ac tivist-Candace-Owens.html. Accessed 4 July 2024.

15 Whittaker, Joe. 'Rethinking Online Radicalization'. Perspectives on Terrorism, vol. 16, no. 4, 2022, www.uni versiteitleiden.nl/binaries/content/assets/customsites/pers pectives-on-terrorism/2022/issue-4/whittaker.pdf. Accessed 6 December 2023.

16 Tufekci, Zeynep. 'YouTube, the Great Radicalizer'. New York Times, 10 March 2018, www.nytimes.com/2018/03/10/opinion/sunday/youtube-politics-radical.html. Accessed 6 December 2022.

17 Fisher, Max, and Amanda Taub. 'On YouTube's Digital Playground, an Open Gate for Pedophiles'. New York Times, 3 June 2019, www.nytimes.com/2019/06/03/world/americas/youtube-pedophiles.html. Accessed 4 July 2024.

18 Daniels, Jessie. 'The Algorithmic Rise of the "Alt-Right"'. Contexts, vol. 17, no. 1, February 2018, pp. 60–65, p. 62, https://doi.org/10.1177/1536504218766547. Accessed 9 October 2024.

19 Bridle, James. 'Something Is Wrong on the Internet'. Medium, 6 November 2017, medium.com/@jamesbridle/something-is-wrong-on-the-internet-c39c471271d2. Accessed 4 July 2024.

20 Bridle, 'Something Is Wrong on the Internet'.

21 Stalinsky, Steven, et al. 'Neo-Nazis and White Supremacists Globally Look to Artificial Intelligence to Promote Their Message, Spread Misinformation, and Aide Their Cause'. Memri.org, 4 June 2024, www.memri.org/dttm/neo-nazis-and-white-supremacists-globally-look-artificial-intelligence-promote-their-message-o. Accessed 4 July 2024.

22 Lewis, Alternative Influence.

23 Moore, Sam, and Alex Roberts. Post-Internet Far Right. Dog Section, 2021, p. 94.

24 Peters, Jeremy W. 'These Conservatives Have a Laser Focus: "Owning the Libs"'. New York Times, 3 August 2020, www.nytimes.com/2020/08/03/us/politics/the-federalist-trump-liberals.html. Accessed 5 July 2024.

25 Melzer, Scott. Gun Crusaders. NYU Press, 2009, p. 59.

26 Blee, Kathleen M. Understanding Racist Activism: Theory, Methods, and Research. Routledge, 2018, p. 71.

27 Kelly, Megan, et al. 'Misogynist Incels and Male Supremacism'. New America, nd, www.newamerica.org/political-reform/reports/misogynist-incels-and-male-supremacism/red-pill-to-black-pill. Accessed 5 July 2024.

28 Leidig, Eviane. The Women of the Far Right. Columbia University Press, 2023.

Notes

29 Southern Poverty Law Center. 'Stormfront'. Southern Poverty Law Center, 2015, www.splcenter.org/fighting-hate/extremist-files/group/stormfront. Accessed 5 July 2024.

30 Southern Poverty Law Center, 'Stormfront'.

31 Daniels, Nice White Ladies: The Truth about White Supremacy, Our Role in It, and How We Can Help Dismantle It. Seal Press, 2021, p. 39.

32 Shah, Areeba. 'Libs of TikTok Owner Chaya Raichik Ramps up Her anti-LGBTQ Crusade'. Salon, 24 January 2023, www.salon.com/2023/01/24/libsof-tiktok-owner-chaya-raichik-ramps-up-her-anti-lgbtq-crusade/. Accessed 29 February 2024.

33 Moore and Roberts, Post-Internet Far Right, p. 159.

34 Gallagher, Aoife, and Tim Squirrell. 'The "Groomer" Slur'. ISD, 16 January 2023, www.isdglobal.org/explainers/the-groomer-slur/. Accessed 5 July 2024.

35 Miller, Cassie. 'Male Supremacy Is at the Core of the Hard Right's Agenda'. Southern Poverty Law Center, 18 April 2023, www.splcenter.org/hatewatch/2023/04/18/male-supremacy-core-hard-rights-agenda. Accessed 5 July 2024.

36 Smith, Laura. 'Lone Wolves Connected Online: A History of Modern White Supremacy'. New York Times, 26 January 2021, www.nytimes.com/2021/01/26/us/louis-beam-white-supremacy-internet.html. Accessed 5 July 2024.

37 Hickey, Cameron. 'TikTok Played a Key Role in MAGA Radicalization'. Wired, 19 March 2021, www.wired.com/story/opinion-tiktok-played-a-key-role-in-maga-radicalization/. Accessed 5 July 2024.

38 Hickey, 'TikTok Played a Key Role in MAGA Radicalization'.

39 Doctor, Nathan, et al. 'NazTok: An Organized Neo-Nazi TikTok Network Is Getting Millions of Views'. ISD Global, 29 June 2024, www.isdglobal.org/digital_dispatches/naztok-an-organized-neo-nazi-tiktok-network-is-getting-millions-of-views/. Accessed 14 August 2024.

40 Bendix, Tom. 'Instagram UK Statistics (2021): Latest Facts and Figures'. Social Films, 25 January 2021, www.socialfilms.co.uk/blog/instagram-uk-statistics. Accessed 5 July 2024.

41 Salty World. 'Algorithmic Bias Report, October 2019'. Salty World, 27 October 2019, saltyworld.net/product/algorithmic-bias-report-october-2019/?_gl=1. Accessed 5 July 2024.

42 Lewis, Alternative Influence, pp. 29–30.

43 Lewis, Alternative Influence, p. 25.

44 Whittaker, 'Rethinking Online Radicalization'.

45 Whittaker, 'Rethinking Online Radicalization', p. 34.

46 Salty World. 'Algorithmic Bias Report'.

47 El-Wardany, Salma. 'Like Our Society, Instagram Is Biased against Women of Colour'. Refinery29.com, 10 December 2020, www.refinery29.com/en-gb/2020/12/10150275/shad ow-ban-instagram-censorship-women-of-colour. Accessed 5 July 2024.

48 Bishop, Sophie. 'The Safety Dance'. Real Life, 11 January 2021, reallifemag.com/the-safety-dance/. Accessed 6 December 2023.

49 Wiley, Danielle. 'How Mom Bloggers Helped Create Influencer Marketing'. AdWeek, 19 March 2018, www. adweek.com/brand-marketing/how-mom-bloggers-helped-create-influencer-marketing/. Accessed 5 July 2024.

50 Miller-Idriss, Cynthia. In Whose Interest? Gender and Far-Right Politics in the United States. Friedrich Ebert Stiftung, 2020, p. 13.

51 Collabstr. '2024 Influencer Marketing Report: Influencer Marketing Statistics, Trends, and Predictions'. Collabstr, 2024, collabstr.com/2024-influencer-marketing-report. Accessed 5 July 2024.

52 Bertoni, Steven. 'Top Creators 2023'. Forbes, 2023, www. forbes.com/sites/stevenbertoni/2023/09/26/top-creators-20 23/. Accessed 29 February 2024.

53 Jennings, Rebecca. 'How the Great Recession Paved the Way for Influencers to Inherit the Earth: Are We All Influencers Now?' Vox, 1 March 2023. www.vox.com/the-goods/23618956/influencer-industry-emily-hund. Accessed 9 October 2024.

54 Florisson, Rebecca, and Olivia Gable. 'The Gender Gap: Insecure Work in the UK'. Lancaster.ac.uk, 19 October 2022, www.lancaster.ac.uk/work-foundation/publications/ the-gender-gap-insecure-work-in-the-uk. Accessed 5 July 2024.

55 Barua, Akrur. 'Gender Equality, Dealt a Blow by COVID-19, Still Has Much Ground to Cover'. Deloitte Insights, 21

January 2022, www2.deloitte.com/uk/en/insights/economy/impact-of-covid-on-women.html. Accessed 29 February 2024.

56 Barua, 'Gender Equality'.

57 Jennings, Rebecca. 'E-Girl Definition: What Is an E-Girl?' Vox, August 2019, www.vox.com/the-goods/2019/8/1/20748707/egirl-definition-what-is-an-eboy. Accessed 6 December 2023.

58 Woodrow, Hazel. 'Feminine Fascism: Girls and Young Women in Hate Subcultures'. Canadian Anti-Hate Education, 22 September 2022, www.antihate.school/femin ine_fascism_girls_and_young_women_in_hate_subcultures. Accessed 18 March 2023.

59 Eisen, Andie. 'Younger Generations May Be Flirting with Christianity'. Coveteur.com, 16 May 2023, coveteur.com/flirting-with-christianity. Accessed 5 July 2024.

60 Olmstead, Molly. 'Uh, Can the NYT Please Not Treat Catholic Reactionaries as a Fun Sexy Trend Story?' Slate, 11 August 2022, slate.com/news-and-politics/2022/08/nyt-dimes-square-trad-catholic-op-ed.html. Accessed 19 March 2023.

61 Sherbert, Biz. 'How Catholicism Became Alt-Fashion's Saviour'. I-D.vice.com, 29 March 2021, i-d.vice.com/en/article/g5b4d9/catholicism-alt-fashion-trend-think-piece.

5 WHAT IS A WOMAN? MAPPING WOMEN'S RADICALISING CONTENT

1 Donovan, Joan, et al. Meme Wars. Bloomsbury, 2022, p. 18.

2 In December of 2023, Kay deleted all her previous videos about being a stay-at-home girlfriend, revealing that she and her boyfriend had broken up.

3 Kay, Kendel. 'I'm a Stay-at-Home Girlfriend. And a Feminist'. Newsweek, 6 March 2023, www.newsweek.com/stay-home-girlfriend-relationships-social-media-1784112. Accessed 5 September 2023.

4 Bruce, Jessica, and Olivia Ryan. 'Attitudes towards Gender Equality'. King's College London, 8 March 2023, www.kcl.ac.uk/giwl/assets/ipsos-giwl-iwd-survey-2023.pdf. Accessed 20 August 2023.

Notes

5 Kitchener, Caroline. 'The Women behind the "Alt-Right"'. The Atlantic, 18 August 2017, www.theatlantic.com/po litics/archive/2017/08/the-women-behind-the-alt-right/53 7168/. Accessed 5 July 2024.

6 Christou, Miranda. '#TradWives: Sexism as Gateway to White Supremacy'. OpenDemocracy, 17 March 2020, www.opendemocracy.net/en/countering-radical-right/trad wives-sexism-gateway-white-supremacy/. Accessed 5 July 2024.

7 Koa Beck. White Feminism. Simon & Schuster Ltd, 2021.

8 Piazza, Jo. 'What the Trad Wives Taught Me about My Own Marriage'. Bustle, 1 February 2024, www.bustle.com/well ness/are-trad-wives-happier. Accessed 17 March 2024.

9 Schaffer, Jennifer. 'The Wife Glitch'. The Baffler, 26 April 2020, thebaffler.com/outbursts/the-wife-glitch-schaffer. Accessed 5 July 2024.

10 Woodrow, Hazel. 'Feminine Fascism: Girls and Young Women in Hate Subcultures'. Canadian Anti-Hate Education, 22 September 2022, www.antihate.school/femin ine_fascism_girls_and_young_women_in_hate_subcultures. Accessed 18 March 2023.

11 Rishab, B. 'How Having a Boyfriend Hurts Female Streamers: The Curious Case of Pokimane, NRG Lulu and More'. Sportskeeda, 13 September 2021, www.sportskeeda.com/ esports/how-boyfriend-hurts-female-streamers-the-curious-case-pokimane-nrg-lulu. Accessed 5 July 2024.

12 Lewis, Sophie. 'The Good Enough Momfluencer'. The Baffler, 18 July 2023, https://thebaffler.com/latest/the-good-enough-momfluencer-lewis. Accessed 23 July 2023.

13 Hu, Zoe. 'The Agoraphobic Fantasy of Tradlife'. Dissent Magazine, 2023, www.dissentmagazine.org/article/the-ago raphobic-fantasy-of-tradlife. Accessed 5 July 2024.

14 Mulhall, Joe. Drums in the Distance. Icon Books, 2021, pp. 35–36.

15 Mulhall, Drums in the Distance.

16 Mudde, Cas. 'Why the Far Right Is Obsessed with "Gender Ideology"'. New Statesman, 8 June 2021, www.newstates man.com/world/2019/09/why-far-right-obsessed-gender-id eology. Accessed 5 July 2024.

Notes

17 Iyer, Prithvi, and Shruti Jain. 'An Unlikely Match: Women and the Far-Right'. Orfonline.org, 4 January 2021, www.orfonline.org/expert-speak/unlikely-match-women-far-right. Accessed 17 March 2024.

18 Boulter, Sophie. 'When Fascism Is Female'. Eurozine.com, 8 October 2022, www.eurozine.com/when-fascism-is-female/. Accessed 6 December 2023.

19 Phipps, Alison. 'White Feminism and the Racial Capitalist Protection Racket: From #MeToo to Me, Not You'. Manchester University Press blog, 2021, https://manchesteruniversitypress.co.uk/blog/2021/05/07/white-feminism-and-the-racial-capitalist-protection-racket-from-metoo-to-me-not-you/. Accessed 9 October 2024.

20 Butler, Judith. 'Why Is the Idea of "Gender" Provoking Backlash the World over?' The Guardian, 23 October 2021, www.theguardian.com/us-news/commentisfree/2021/oct/23/judith-butler-gender-ideology-backlash. Accessed 6 July 2024.

21 Burns, Katelyn. 'TERFs: The Rise of "Trans-Exclusionary Radical Feminists", Explained'. Vox, 5 September 2019, www.vox.com/identities/2019/9/5/20840101/terfs-radical-feminists-gender-critical. Accessed 6 July 2024.

22 This is a very brief overview, as the history of TERF and its implications is vast and complex and has been explored far more expertly by feminist scholars in dedicated texts.

23 Lewis, Sophie. 'Opinion: How British Feminism Became Anti-Trans'. New York Times, 7 February 2019, www.nytimes.com/2019/02/07/opinion/terf-trans-women-britain.html. Accessed 28 August 2023.

24 Phipps, Me, Not You, p. 135.

25 Tudor, Alyosxa. 'Terfism Is White Distraction: On BLM, Decolonising the Curriculum, anti-Gender Attacks and Feminist Transphobia'. Engenderings, 19 June 2020, blogs.lse.ac.uk/gender/2020/06/19/terfism-is-white-distraction-on-blm-decolonising-the-curriculum-anti-gender-attacks-and-feminist-transphobia/. Accessed 6 July 2024.

26 Lewis, 'Opinion'.

27 Miller, Edie. 'Why Is British Media so Transphobic?' The Outline, 5 November 2018, http://theoutline.com/

post/6536/british-feminists-media-transphobic. Accessed 6 July 2024.

28 Miller, 'Why Is British Media so Transphobic?'.

29 Balci, Utkucan et al. 'Beyond Fish and Bicycles: Exploring the Varieties of Online Women's Ideological Spaces'. UCL Discovery (University College London), 30 April 2023, https://doi.org/10.1145/3578503.3583618. Accessed 29 September 2024.

30 Center on Extremism. 'What Is "Grooming?" The Truth behind the Dangerous, Bigoted Lie Targeting the LGBTQ+ Community'. Adl.org, 16 September 2022, www.adl.org/resources/blog/what-grooming-truth-behind-dangerous-bigoted-lie-targeting-lgbtq-community. Accessed 6 July 2024.

31 Breland, Ali. 'Why Are Right-Wing Conspiracies so Obsessed with Pedophilia?' Mother Jones, August 2019, www.motherjones.com/politics/2019/07/why-are-right-wing-conspiracies-so-obsessed-with-pedophilia/. Accessed 3 September 2023.

32 Maza, Carlos. 'Debunking the Big Myth about Transgender-Inclusive Bathrooms'. Media Matters for America, 20 March 2014, www.mediamatters.org/fox-nation/debunking-big-myth-about-transgender-inclusive-bathrooms. Accessed 6 July 2024.

33 Evans, Holly. 'Italy Begins Removing Gay Mothers from Children's Birth Certificates'. The Independent, 20 July 2023, www.independent.co.uk/news/world/europe/italy-gay-mothers-birth-certificates-lgtbq-b2378622.html. Accessed 6 July 2024.

34 Butler, 'Why Is the Idea of "Gender" Provoking Backlash the World over?'.

35 Reuters. 'LGBTQ Italians on Alert as Right-Wing Alliance Triumphs in Election'. NBC News, 27 September 2022, www.nbcnews.com/nbc-out/out-politics-and-policy/lgbtq-italians-alert-right-wing-alliance-triumphs-election-rcna49593. Accessed 14 August 2024.

36 Butler, 'Why Is the Idea of "Gender" Provoking Backlash the World over?'.

37 Classically Abby. 'The Real Body Positivity: Adele Looks Fantastic – Healthy Is Beautiful!' Youtube.com,

www.youtube.com/watch?v=e2o8Jn8AFqM. Accessed 6 December 2023.

38 Mrs Midwest. 'Let's Talk about Body Positivity'. Youtube. com, 19 July 2019, www.youtube.com/watch?v=PSFl5poftoo. Accessed 6 December 2023.

39 Dee, Katherine. 'Being Fit Is Far-Right Now, Apparently'. UnHerd, 11 July 2023, http://unherd.com/thepost/being-fit-is-far-right-now-apparently/. Accessed 6 July 2024.

40 Copeland, Carolyn. 'Fatphobia: Where It Comes from, Why It Happens, and How It Hurts Women of Color the Most'. Daily Kos, 15 June 2020, www.dailykos.com/stor ies/2020/6/15/1950249/-Fatphobia-where-it-comes-from-w hy-it-happens-and-how-it-hurts-women-of-color-the-most. Accessed 23 July 2023.

41 Lerman, Kristina, et al. 'Radicalized by Thinness: Using a Model of Radicalization to Understand pro-Anorexia Communities on Twitter'. ResearchGate, May 2023, www. researchgate.net/publication/370937848_Radicalized_by_ Thinness_Using_a_Model_of_Radicalization_to_Understa nd_Pro-Anorexia_Communities_on_Twitter. Accessed 6 July 2024.

42 Center for Countering Digital Hate. 'Deadly by Design'. Counterhate.com, 15 December 2022, counterhate.com/ research/deadly-by-design/. Accessed 6 July 2024.

43 Darby, Seyward. Sisters in Hate: American Women on the Front Lines of White Nationalism. Little Brown and Company, 2020.

44 Sudjic, Olivia. '"I Felt Colossally Naive": The Backlash against the Birth Control App'. The Guardian, 23 July 2018, www.theguardian.com/society/2018/jul/21/colossally-nai ve-backlash-birth-control-app. Accessed 6 July 2024.

45 Muir, Kate. 'The Pill's Effects on Women Can Be Devastating: We Need Better Information, Now'. The Observer, 11 June 2023, www.theguardian.com/society/commentisfree/2023/ jun/11/the-pills-effects-on-women-can-be-devastating-we-need-better-information-now. Accessed 6 July 2024; Swift, Bethan, and Christian Becker. 'Birth Control Continues to Fail Women – so Why Has Nothing Changed?' The Conversation, 14 July 2021, http://theconversation.com/

birth-control-continues-to-fail-women-so-why-has-nothing-changed-164195. Accessed 6 July 2024.

46 Byrne, Anna. 'How to Close the Gender Health Gap'. Wired, 24 May 2023, www.wired.co.uk/article/womens-health-care-inequalities. Accessed 11 August 2023.

47 Daniels, Jessie. Nice White Ladies: The Truth about White Supremacy, Our Role in It, and How We Can Help Dismantle It. Seal Press, 2021.

48 Norris, Sian. Bodies under Siege. Verso, 2023.

49 Edmund Burke Foundation. 'Homepage'. Edmund Burke Foundation, nd, https://burke.foundation/. Accessed 6 July 2024.

50 Norris, Bodies under Siege, p. 155.

51 Browne, Kath, and Catherine J. Nash. 'The Rise of Heteroactivism'. Rte.ie, 22 February 2018, www.rte.ie/brainstorm/2018/0222/942632-the-rise-of-heteroactivism/. Accessed 6 July 2024.

52 Abderemane, Assad. 'Reframing "Mother Nature" in the Wake of Misogynistic Climate Denialism'. Lady Science, 20 February 2020, www.ladyscience.com/features/reframing-mother-nature-misogynistic-climate-denialism. Accessed 23 August 2023.

53 Brough, Aaron R., et al. 'Is Eco-Friendly Unmanly? The Green-Feminine Stereotype and Its Effect on Sustainable Consumption'. Journal of Consumer Research, vol. 43, no. 4, 4 August 2016, pp. 567–582, academic.oup.com/jcr/article/43/4/567/2630509, https://doi.org/10.1093/jcr/ucw044. Accessed 6 July 2024.

54 Maisonnave, Fabiano. 'Amazon Deforestation in Brazil Remains near 15-Year High'. AP News, 30 November 2022, http://apnews.com/article/jair-bolsonaro-forests-brazil-middle-east-deforestation-863224be226725da06db7768b305c3ea. Accessed 6 July 2024.

55 Shadijanova, Diyora. 'What Is Eco-Fascism and Why Is It Dangerous?' The Face, 18 October 2021, http://theface.com/society/eco-fascism-ideology-climate-change-white-supremacy-co2-emissions-pollution. Accessed 27 August 2023.

56 Hancock, Elaina. 'A Darker Shade of Green: Understanding Ecofascism'. UConn Today, 7 September 2022, http://today.

uconn.edu/2022/09/a-darker-shade-of-green/#. Accessed 27 August 2023.

57 Forchtner, Bernhard. 'Eco-fascism: Justifications of Terrorist Violence in the Christchurch Mosque Shooting and the El Paso Shooting'. OpenDemocracy, 13 August 2019. www. opendemocracy.net/en/countering-radical-right/eco-fascism-justifications-terrorist-violence-christchurch-mosque-shooti ng-and-el-paso-shooting/. Accessed 10 October 2024.

58 Nineteenth-century economist Thomas Malthus believed that human population growth was potentially exponential but that supply of other resources, namely food, was not, meaning that eventually humans would outstrip the amount of food we can produce, leading to a decline in birth rates and ultimately a breakdown of society.

59 United States Holocaust Memorial Museum. 'Origins of Neo-Nazi and White Supremacist Terms and Symbols: A Glossary'. Ushmm.org, 2017, www.ushmm.org/antisem itism/what-is-antisemitism/origins-of-neo-nazi-and-white-supremacist-terms-and-symbols. Accessed 6 July 2024.

60 Sowemimo, Annabel. 'Ecofascism Is Infiltrating the Conversation around Reproductive Rights'. *Novara Media*, 18 February 2022, novaramedia.com/2022/02/18/ecofasci sm-is-infilitrating-the-conversation-around-reproductive-ri ghts/. Accessed 22 February 2022.

6 WHITE SHARIA NOW: WOMEN'S EXPERIENCES IN FAR-RIGHT COMMUNITIES

1 Mattheis, Ashley. 'Shieldmaidens of Whiteness: (Alt) Maternalism and Women Recruiting for the Far/Alt-Right'. Journal for Deradicalization, no. 17, 23 December 2018, pp. 128–162, journals.sfu.ca/jd/index.php/jd/article/ view/177. Accessed 4 July 2024.

2 Harrington, Mary. 'Lauren Southern: How My Tradlife Turned Toxic'. UnHerd, 5 May 2024, http://unherd.com/20 24/05/lauren-southern-the-tradlife-influencer-filled-with-re gret/. Accessed 6 July 2024.

3 Harrington, 'Lauren Southern'.

4 Bates, Lydia. 'Patriarchal Violence: Misogyny from the Far

Right to the Mainstream'. Southern Poverty Law Center, 1 February 2021, www.splcenter.org/news/2021/02/01/patri archal-violence-misogyny-far-right-mainstream. Accessed 28 September 2023.

5 Llanera, Tracy. 'The Misogyny Paradox and the Alt-Right'. Hypatia, 17 March 2023, pp. 1–20, https://doi.org/10.1017/ hyp.2023.4. Accessed 1 April 2023.

6 Llanera, 'The Misogyny Paradox and the Alt-Right'.

7 Hackman, Rose. 'Femicides in the US: The Silent Epidemic Few Dare to Name'. The Guardian, 26 September 2021, www.theguardian.com/us-news/2021/sep/26/femicide-us-silent-epidemic. Accessed 6 July 2024.

8 Chowcat, Anna. 'Refuge Responds to ONS Domestic Abuse Data'. Refuge, 24 November 2023, http://refuge.org.uk/ne ws/refuge-responds-to-ons-domestic-abuse-data/. Accessed 6 July 2024.

9 Reeve, Elle. 'How Women Fall into America's White Power Movement'. CNN, 30 October 2019, edition.cnn. com/2019/10/30/us/white-supremacist-woman-reeve/index. html. Accessed 6 July 2024.

10 Reeve, 'How Women Fall into America's White Power Movement'.

11 Dodgson, Lindsay. 'As Andrew Tate Languishes in Jail, a New Celebrity anti-Feminist Creator Is Filling the Gap. Unlike Him, She's a Woman'. Insider, 22 March 2023, www.insider.com/the-rise-of-pearl-the-female-misogynist-andrew-tate-2023-3. Accessed 13 October 2023.

12 Dickson, E. J. 'How Do Women Become White Supre-macists?' Rolling Stone, 15 July 2020, www.rollingstone. com/culture/culture-features/seyward-darby-sisters-in-hate-female-white-supremacists-1029109/. Accessed 10 October 2024.

13 Blee, Kathleen, et al. 'Why Do Women Leave the Far-Right?'. Center for Research on Extremism, 2018, www.sv.uio. no/c-rex/english/news-and-events/right-now/2018/why-do-women-leave-the-far-right.html. Accessed 9 October 2023.

14 Blee, et al. 'Why Do Women Leave the Far-Right?'.

15 Darby, Seyward. 'White Supremacy Was Her World: And Then She Left'. New York Times, 17 July 2020, www.ny

times.com/2020/07/17/opinion/sunday/white-supremacy-hate-movements.html. Accessed 5 November 2023.

16 Blee, et al. 'Why Do Women Leave the Far-Right?'.

17 Blee, et al. 'Why Do Women Leave the Far-Right?'.

18 Smith, Erika W. 'What Happens to the Stay-at-Home Girlfriend after a Breakup?' Cosmopolitan, 25 March 2024, www.cosmopolitan.com/uk/love-sex/relationships/a60293524/stay-at-home-girlfriend-tik-tok-trend-breakups/. Accessed 6 July 2024.

7 WHICH WAY WESTERN WOMAN? ADDRESSING THE FUTURE OF WOMEN IN THE FAR RIGHT

1 Valasik, Matthew, and Shannon Reid. 'After the Insurrection, America's Far-Right Groups Get More Extreme'. Salon, 21 March 2021, www.salon.com/2021/03/21/after-the-insurrection-americas-far-right-groups-get-more-extreme_partner/. Accessed 5 November 2023.

2 Reeve, Elle. 'How Women Fall into America's White Power Movement'. CNN, 30 October 2019, http://edition.cnn.com/2019/10/30/us/white-supremacist-woman-reeve/index.html. Accessed 6 July 2024.

3 Moore, Sam, and Alex Roberts. Post-Internet Far Right. Dog Section, 2021, p. 146.

4 Wolfe-Robinson, Maya. 'Guide to Spotting Far-Right Extremism Sent to Schools in England and Wales'. The Guardian, 2 March 2021, www.theguardian.com/uk-news/2021/mar/02/guide-to-spotting-far-right-extremism-sent-to-schools-in-england-and-wales. Accessed 10 March 2024.

5 Smith, Matthew. 'One in Six Boys Aged 6–15 Have a Positive View of Andrew Tate'. Yougov.co.uk, 27 September 2023, yougov.co.uk/society/articles/47419-one-in-six-boys-aged-6–15-have-a-positive-view-of-andrew-tate. Accessed 10 March 2024.

6 Leidig, Eviane. The Women of the Far Right. Columbia University Press, 2023.

7 Llanera, Tracy. 'The Misogyny Paradox and the Alt-Right'. Hypatia, 17 March 2023, pp. 1–20, https://doi.org/10.1017/hyp.2023.4. Accessed 1 April 2023.

Notes

8 Lorenz, Taylor. 'Meet the Woman Working to Stop the Far-Right Creator Money Machine'. Washington Post, 13 December 2023, www.washingtonpost.com/technology/2023/12/13/nandini-jammi-alex-jones-demonetization/. Accessed 7 July 2024.

9 Lattin, Pesach. 'Nandini Jammi: The Woman Who Cost Breitbart 90% of Its Ad Revenue and Exposed Pubmatic's Support for Hate Speech and Disinformation'. ADOTAT with Pesach Lattin, 12 September 2023, www.adotat.com/2023/09/nandini-jammi-the-woman-who-cost-breitbart-90-of-its-ad-revenue-and-exposed-pubmatics-support-for-hate-speech-and-disinformation/. Accessed 7 July 2024.

10 Savolainen, Laura. 'The Shadow Banning Controversy: Perceived Governance and Algorithmic Folklore'. Media, Culture & Society, vol. 44, no. 6, 12 March 2022, pp. 1091–1109, https://doi.org/10.1177/01634437221077174. Accessed 6 July 2024.

11 Whittaker, Joe, et al. 'Recommender Systems and the Amplification of Extremist Content'. Internet Policy Review, vol. 10, no. 2, 30 June 2021, policyreview.info/articles/analysis/recommender-systems-and-amplification-extremist-content. Accessed 6 July 2024.

12 Whittaker, 'Recommender Systems and the Amplification of Extremist Content'.

13 Daniels, Jessie. 'The Algorithmic Rise of the "Alt-Right"'. Contexts, vol. 17, no. 1, February 2018, pp. 60–65, http://journals.sagepub.com/doi/10.1177/1536504218766547, https://doi.org/10.1177/1536504218766547. Accessed 6 July 2024.

14 Phipps, Alison. 'From "Sex-Based Rights" to "Become Ungovernable": From Supremacy to Solidarity'. Phipps.space, 12 May 2022, phipps.space/2022/05/12/sex-based-rights/. Accessed 6 July 2024.

Index

Titles of books can be found after authors' names.
'n.' after a page number indicates the number of a note on that page.

Index

Index

Index

Index

Index

Index

Index

Index

Index

white men
  alt-right 32–3
  internet culture 57–8
  patriarchy 57–8, 85–9,
    160–1
  sexual violence 87, 160–1
white nationalists
  alt-right 31
  appeal to women 125–6
  neo-Nazi content on
    TikTok 129–30
  teenage girls and #Thinspo
    content 142
  underestimation of women
    50
  women's intrinsic value
    as wives and mothers
    35–6
whiteness, and victimhood
    8, 160
white-pilling 122
white sharia 199
white supremacists
  compared with tradcaths
    140
  Identity Europa 198–9
  instrumental role of white
    women 5, 35
  language of alt-right 31
  masters of tailoring content
    116
  spread of beliefs online by
    algorithms 110
  subordination of recruits 91
  white women's
    empowerment and
    family values 41
  women who see themselves
    as feminists 126

white womanhood 5, 46, 126,
    148
white women 2–3
  as birthers of the nation 35,
    76–7
  and Black women in
    tradwife content
    148–9
  favoured by Instagram
    133
  Ku Klux Klan (KKK)
    41–2
  racism and sexism 27
  right to vote in USA 46
  voting for Trump 26–8
  see also domesticity and
    domestic labour;
    patriarchy
Whittaker, Joe 109, 132
Whyte, Lara 50
Wilkinson, Abi 98
wojaks 74, 89–90, 199–200
womanhood
  biblical 69, 106, 132, 151
  traditional 13, 115, 121
  white 5, 46, 126, 148
women
  as actual people 227–8
  arguments to dissuade from
    far right 8–9
  attitudes to and beliefs of
    far right
    as commodities 52
    control of sexual and
      bodily autonomy 88
    domesticity in alt-right
      views 61–2
    as helpmeets in biblical
      womanhood 151

277

EU authorised representative for GPSR:
Easy Access System Europe, Mustamäe tee 50,
10621 Tallinn, Estonia
gpsr.requests@easproject.com

www.ingramcontent.com/pod-product-compliance
Lightning Source LLC
Chambersburg PA
CBHW031426270326
41930CB00007B/585